Magnolias CLASSIC SOUTHERN CUISINE

COLLECTED RECIPES FROM THE HEART OF CHARLESTON

DON DRAKE

Photographs by John D. Smoak III

Gibbs Smith

First Edition

27 26 25 24 23   5 4 3 2 1

Text © 2023 Don Drake and Hospitality Management Group, Inc.
Photographs © 2023 John D. Smoak III

Published by
Gibbs Smith
P.O. Box 667
Layton, Utah 84041

1.800.835.4993 orders
www.gibbs-smith.com

Designed by Ryan Thomann and Renee Bond
Printed and bound in China by RR Donnelley Asia Printing Solutions
Gibbs Smith books are printed on either recycled, 100% post-consumer
waste, FSC-certified papers or on paper produced from sustainable PEFC-
certified forest/controlled wood source. Learn more at www.pefc.org.

Library of Congress Control Number: 2023008955
ISBN: 978-1-4236-6400-0

Contents

Acknowledgments

SINCE MAGNOLIAS' OPENING IN 1990, around 6,420,000 people have joined us for lunch and dinner. We are grateful for your business! Also, about 1,700 people have come to work with us over the past thirty-some-odd years. These employees—bringing their personalities, passions, minds, and talents—all come together on a daily basis to create the lively, bustling work environment and ambiance that is Magnolias. Our great staff is truly the heartbeat of the restaurant.

A special thank-you to the Parsell family: TJ, Louisa, Suzi, and the late Tom Sr.

The Magnolias' alumni—there are many. Every one of you has left your mark on the restaurant and our hearts, and we thank you.

Mary Forlano: I can't say enough about her continued direction and encouragement—especially keeping me on time with deadlines. I would have been lost without Mary's incredible organizational skills! Thank you.

Diane Howard, our longtime general manager, for her sense of humor, intelligence, friendship, energy, and patience.

The Magnolias "Incredible Six," our chefs who have all helped celebrate the wins and weather the storms for the past two decades: James, Landice and Delon Simmons, Kevin Southerlin, Marshall Tucker, and Travis Smalls.

To my pastry chef, Jen Mains, for her creative talents in writing recipes and making sure they work. Jen is always my sounding board for current topics.

To our present kitchen staff, who hold down the fort every day: Damon North, Josh Taylor, Ms. Roe Garnett, Jerod Durant, and Cliff Washington.

Thank you again to the fabulous staff at Magnolias—past and present—all of our chefs, sous chefs, butchers, managers, hosts, wait staff, bartenders, pastry cooks, prep staff, and dish crew. We are so fortunate to have you as part of our team.

To John Smoak and Anne Pope, for making sure the pictures and manuscript got to the publisher on time.

To my family: My wife, Martha, and sons, Marshall and Travis, for their many years of support and understanding about a chef's work-life and schedule. Thank you for being by my side on this journey.

Foreword

IT WAS 1989, AND THE CITY OF CHARLESTON was recovering from the aftermath of the devastation of Hurricane Hugo when my late father, Tom Parsell, purchased an old historic building in the French Quarter district—in fact, the site of the city's original Custom House in 1739. Despite the Quarter having become a rundown part of town in the preceding years, he had a vision to reinvigorate the area with a traditional Lowcountry fine-dining restaurant. Magnolias opened soon after that, in 1990, igniting a local culinary renaissance and paving the way for restaurants in Charleston—and across the South—with its upscale Southern cuisine.

As I reflect on the last three decades at Magnolias, I think of its long history of serving countless meals, the people, the stories, and the many celebrations that we have shared with our patrons. I am also humbled by the significance of Magnolias' role in the evolution of Charleston's restaurant landscape for both locals and the burgeoning tourism industry. Magnolias was a key player in the city's post-Hugo revival and helped put Charleston on the map as a premier culinary destination in the South. Having grown up in Charleston, maintaining a sense of true Charleston character is very important to me. I believe that we have succeeded in that endeavor and continue to thrive because of that special character.

Since 1991, executive chef Don Drake has been the driving force behind Magnolias' ability to perpetuate the impeccable bar that was set early on. His passion for food and hospitality continues to keep Magnolias at the top of its game, and I salute his dedication. Most of all, I appreciate his partnership and friendship through these years.

The last few years have been a trying time for everyone, particularly those in the hospitality industry. To go along with the difficulties presented by the pandemic, Magnolias suffered a debilitating fire that led to a six-month closure. Having persevered through these hardships, Chef Drake and I felt that a new cookbook incorporating classic recipes of our prior cookbooks with new recipes created since the last book was published in 2015 was the right way to celebrate our ability to come through these recent trials stronger than ever. Our hope is that you will find recipes and inspiration that will create as many special memories in your own kitchen as they have given to us at Magnolias.

—*TJ Parsell, President/Owner*
Hospitality Management Group, Inc.

Introduction

CAN A BOOK BE ABOUT EATING MEMORIES?
We have a lot of them at Magnolias, looking back through the years: helping loyal patrons and friends with birthday celebrations, anniversaries, marriage proposals, first dates, new businesses, and graduations. I've gotten some outrageous requests from guests, but we make them happen!

I love hearing people share their Magnolias memories: stories about what they had to eat, who they dined with, and what the occasion was. It's amazing the details they remember—down to the wine they drank, where they were seated, and the waiter who served them. When someone tells me what they had to eat, I can usually give them a year they were last here.

Some of our original customers whom I've become friends with are getting up there in age. In fact, we have an unofficial VIP birthday club at the restaurant with about a dozen or so of our guests who stop in for their birthday lunch every year. We call them the "90 and Over" club—the oldest friend is 102 this year—and it's my honor to treat these special folks to lunch on their birthdays. We have great conversations talking about cooking and what things they have seen and experienced during their lifetimes. The kids and grandkids will tell me that their mom or dad *insisted* they take them down to the Magnolias for their birthday! Memories like these make Magnolias the special place it's become for so many over the decades.

For *Magnolias Classic Southern Cuisine*, we chose to include our most-requested recipes along with a few of our favorite newer dishes. Each one of them brings many memories of an era in time, the employees who worked with us, and the special customers who dined with us. Working toward our fourth decade now at Magnolias, the early years seem to slip past with time itself. A couple of you reading this book might ask how we got started. I thought I should briefly explain it: In 1989, businessman Thomas Parsell Sr. had the foresight to purchase Charleston's original 1739 Custom House building located in the historic French Quarter section of town. Hurricane Hugo had come through as a Category 5 hurricane in the fall of the previous year, leaving a wake of destruction in its path. The area was in desperate need of someone to come in and rehabilitate the neighborhood, and Tom and his partners had the vision.

In the summer of 1990 and after extensive renovations, Magnolias was ready to open. It was an immediate hit and brought people back downtown, forever changing the French Quarter. Magnolias took old "Charleston Receipts" and gave them a new life. We were the first to put grits on the dinner menu! We bought our produce from local farmers, seafood from local boats, and wonderful artisan grits from local mills. We got our pigs out of Georgia and did our own butchering. Magnolias was doing "farm-to-table" before the sentence was even thought of—and at a time it was not necessarily cool to do so. Looking across American restaurants today you see many of our early ideas spread throughout the country. Many print and media publications give Magnolias accolades for being an early pioneer of the Southern food movement.

That said, I would like to acknowledge some of the great Charleston restaurateurs that came before us and taught many of us about food and wine. My family and I arrived in Charleston in 1990. As a newcomer, I asked a couple of longtime friends, Jack Limehouse and his wife, Andrea, to share who led the way for us. Jack's dad, H. B. Limehouse, opened a produce stand in 1945 right downtown on Market Street. Jack took over the business when his father passed away in 1972 and we still do business with Limehouse Produce today. He told me there were a few established restaurants in town at that time: the Colony House, Perdita's, the Cavallaro, Everett's, the Goodie House, Kitty's Fine Foods, and Henry's on the Market.

Later that decade and into the 1980s, with a newly elected mayor by the name of Joe Riley and a new international arts festival called "Spoleto," the city saw an influx of European investment in the downtown area. The following group of entrepreneurs led the charge: Franz Meier, Chris Weiss, and Henry Paddington took over the Colony House; Serge Clair opened Marianne's; Heinz Poke and Hans Berringer opened the Cotton Exchange and the Fish Market; Alain Saley opened Le Midi; Jose de Anceleto and Phillip Million opened Restaurant Million; Robert Dixon opened Robert's of Charleston; and John Sutcliffe and Kiara Balish opened Garibaldi's. All the above restaurants are now closed except one, Henry's. Many of these chefs and restaurant owners had a major influence on their young employees who are in the food scene now. We came from the original entrepreneurs. They taught us well: We listened, we watched, and we learned the old ways.

Magnolias has stood the test of time, accomplishing what only a handful of other restaurants have done. My time, like many of the chefs mentioned, will come to a close in the next couple of years. I hope to be handing the reins off to one of the accomplished apprentices that have stood with me through thick and thin over the years. I know what Magnolias and our patrons have meant to them and I hope the staff knows the pleasure I've had working with *them* over the years, watching them grow into the chefs and restaurateurs of tomorrow. I hope you enjoy this book as a tribute to Magnolias' place in the history of Charleston's fabulous food scene.

Now put on your apron—it's time to start cooking!

COOKING TOOLS
and
TECHNIQUES

THERE IS A NEW TURN IN THE SOUTH
taking place in kitchens across America.
You will find Southern restaurants from
Washington State to Maine, everyone putting
their unique twist on their interpretation of
what "Southern food" means. I want to help
you on your new journey with classic Southern
food, giving you some basic techniques and
cooking science that might help.

Let's start with measuring. Fannie Farmer
was the first to emphasize measurements
with her first book, *The Boston Cooking-School
Cookbook*, published in 1896. Prior to that, I
think most measurements were just by sight.
Professional chefs prefer weighted measurements to volume since it's more precise. When
purchasing measuring equipment, you need
four things: dry measuring cups, wet measuring cups, measuring spoons, and a food scale.

How do you know what kind you're buying? A liquid measuring cup is generally made
of glass or plastic and is clear with markings on
the sides. They have handles with pour spouts.
Dry measuring cups are generally made of

metal or plastic and have long handles with
flat tops that make it easy to sweep off excess
sugar or flour.

Moving on to measuring spoons: Get a
good metal set. It should include 1 tablespoon,
1 teaspoon, $1/2$ teaspoon, $1/4$ teaspoon, and
$1/8$ teaspoon. When it comes to using your
measuring spoons, try to remember this:
1 tablespoon equals 3 teaspoons; 4 tablespoons
equal $1/4$ cup. That will help you scale a recipe
up or down. If you're going to do a lot of baking, I recommend you buy a reliable scale that
does both metric and imperial measurements.
The next requirements are a good set of knives,
cookware, and a good food thermometer.

Some general assumptions about
temperatures when using this book: "Room
temperature" is about 70 degrees F. "Chilled"
is considered between 35 and 40 degrees F.
Flour and grains are to be assumed at room
temperature. If the flour is cold from being
stored in the refrigerator, let it sit out on the
counter for 30 minutes before using. Eggs are
assumed to be chilled. If you need to bring
your eggs to room temperature, place them in
a bowl of warm water for 5 minutes. Butter is
chilled unless otherwise noted. Softened butter
is between 60 and 68 degrees F. Chicken, fish,
and meat are chilled unless otherwise noted.
You want to keep them below 40 degrees F.

Salt: There is a big difference between
types and measurements. We use Diamond
Crystal kosher salt in our kitchen at Magnolias
because of its open crystal structure. If you
compared Morton's kosher salt to Diamond
Crystal, the measurements would be $2\,1/4$
teaspoons Morton's to 3 teaspoons of Diamond
Crystal. Also, 3 teaspoons of Diamond Crystal
kosher salt would equal $1\,1/2$ teaspoons of
ordinary table salt. Please keep this in mind
when following the recipes.

When using fresh herbs, add the more
robust herbs like thyme, rosemary, sage, and
oregano to your recipes early in the cooking

process. Add the more delicate herbs like chives, dill, parsley, tarragon, and basil at the end. They tend to lose their flavor and color quickly.

When most of us learned about the four primary taste buds, it was sweet, salty, bitter, and sour. Now there's a fifth one called "umami," which comes mostly from MSG additives or naturally from fruits and vegetables high in a common amino acid called "glutamine." Remember the shaker of Accent in your mom's cupboard? For more of a natural umami taste, try adding anchovies, soy sauce, or Worcestershire sauce; all are heavy with glutamine. Also, next time, instead of heading for the saltshaker, try adding a little vinegar or lemon juice to a dish. The acid will really brighten up the dish!

When seasoning with black pepper, if you want that strong, assertive bite, season after you have seared the protein. For a less pungent taste, season before cooking. The heat has a big effect on black pepper. When adding salt, always sprinkle it about 10 inches away from the dish—it helps eliminate salty spots that occur when the dish hasn't been mixed well. And remember one of the most important pieces of advice: People eat with their eyes first. Make it look good!

How do you know if the meat is cooked? A lot of us old-timers do it by time. That technique is not always accurate, hence the list of temperatures below. I am going to take into account "resting" the protein and the cooking that carries over. "Carry-over time" means the meat is going to continue to cook for another 5 to 10 minutes while it rests. When cooking large roasts, steaks, and chops, take the carryover time into consideration.

Note: Carry-over time doesn't apply to birds and seafood. Always cook your poultry and fish to the desired degree of doneness.

- Rare beef or lamb: Stop cooking at 115 to 120 degrees F.
- Medium-rare beef or lamb: Stop cooking at 120 to 125 degrees F.
- Medium beef or lamb: Stop cooking at 130 to 135 degrees F.
- Medium-well beef or lamb: Stop cooking at 140 to 145 degrees F.
- Well-done beef or lamb: Stop cooking at 150 to 155 degrees F.
- Medium pork: Stop cooking at 140 to 145 degrees F.
- Well-done pork: Stop cooking at 150 to 155 degrees F.

My last piece of advice is on brining. It accomplishes three things: It helps the meat retain moisture, making it juicier; it helps the meat become tender; and finally, unlike the method of sprinkling on the salt and pepper, the brine penetrates deeper into the meat and produces a well-seasoned product.

- Whole turkey (12 to 17 pounds): 2 gallons cold water, 1 cup salt; brine for 10 hours
- Whole turkey (18 to 24 pounds): 3 gallons cold water, $1\frac{1}{2}$ cups salt; brine for 12 hours
- Bone-in turkey breast: 1 gallon cold water, $\frac{1}{2}$ cup salt; brine for 5 hours
- Whole chicken (3 to 5 pounds): 2 quarts cold water, $\frac{1}{2}$ cup salt; brine for 1 hour
- Whole chicken (5 to 8 pounds): 3 quarts cold water, $\frac{3}{4}$ cup salt; brine for 1 hour
- Bone-in chicken pieces (4 pounds): 2 quarts cold water, $\frac{1}{2}$ cup salt; brine for 45 minutes
- Bone-in pork chops: $1\frac{1}{2}$ quarts cold water, 3 tablespoons salt; brine for 1 hour
- Pork roast (3 to 6 pounds): 2 quarts cold water, $\frac{1}{4}$ cup salt; brine for 90 minutes

You will never know if you don't try new things, so experiment! Have fun in the kitchen. Feel free to change the recipes to fit your own style of cooking and tastes.

The

PANTRY

Pickled Vegetables

Most Southerners have a favorite brand of pickles. Quite a few food enthusiasts make their own and don't stop there; they pickle all kinds of assorted vegetables, moving on to eggs and meats. Take, for instance, the bright-pink pigs' feet that you find every now and then at that country store or gas station. You've seen them sitting in the big jars on the cash register counter in that strange pink pickling solution, sometimes with sausages and eggs. I've tried the eggs but haven't been brave enough to sample the sausage or pigs' feet!

I am a big fan of pickling and fermentation. In Magnolias' kitchen, we use a pickling brine for seasonal vegetables and a standard brine for ham, turkey, pork, and seafood. We also use fermentation when making collard green kimchi, Brussels sprouts, or cabbage sauerkrauts. When it comes to pickles, we have two different brines, one for spring/summer produce and one for fall/winter produce.

A couple of pointers: When you blanch vegetables, make sure to add salt to your blanching water. Also try adding a little salt to your iced water that you shock your vegetables in. You'll be amazed at the difference. When we use cabbage, tomatoes, cucumbers, eggplant, and various other vegetables, we sprinkle a slight salt cure on the vegetables to pull some of the moisture out of the product, and place it on a rack to drain. We then rinse it off, pat dry, and pickle it.

When we brine, we're trying to retain moisture and add flavor. When we cure a product, we are trying to remove the moisture from the product. That is the big difference between the two. Most novice pickle makers start out with the 3-2-1 method. It's an easy, mostly foolproof method, and it produces good results that are a little on the sweet side. For example: 3/4 cup sugar, 1/2 cup water, 1/4 cup vinegar. Bring it all to a boil until the sugar dissolves. Fill your jars with the vegetables you want to pickle, then pour the solution into the jars with your vegetables. Add any additional condiments, such as dill, bay leaves, garlic, hot peppers, mustard seeds, and turmeric. Let it sit overnight to cool, and then it will be ready to eat.

Here are a few more complicated varieties of pickled vegetables for both spring/summer and fall/winter produce. All will assume you start out with a hot-water bath for your jars and that they are cleaned and sterilized.

Hot-Water Bath Canning Method

First, assemble your supplies: glass jars (mostly pints and quarts), caps and bands, and a large stockpot that will hold a rack in the bottom (or use a boiling-water canner). Jars can't rest on the bottom of the pot because they'll burst. You'll need a pot that is deep and wide enough to cover the jars with an inch or two of water. You'll also need

continued »

measuring cups and spoons, a wide-mouth funnel, a chopstick for air pockets, a jar lifter, a set of tongs, clean dish towels, and a ladle.

Inspect the caps and screw-on bands for damage, and heat the oven to 200 degrees F. Place the jars on their sides in the stockpot or canner, and fill the pot with enough water to cover the jars by at least 1 to 2 inches. Bring to a boil and then reduce to a simmer. Remove the jars, tilting slightly to let the water run back into the pot. Place the jars in a large roasting pan and put them in the preheated oven until ready for use.

Fill a medium-size pot halfway with water and bring to a boil, then reduce heat to a simmer and add the bands and caps. Do not boil the caps. Let the bands and caps sit in the water until ready to use. Carefully remove the jars from the oven, placing the jars and the stockpot on a flat surface. Use the wide-mouth funnel to fill the jars, allowing for headspace as directed in the recipes. Carefully remove the

funnel and use the chopstick to remove any visible air pockets. When the jars are filled, wipe the jar rims clean and remove the caps from the water using a set of small tongs. Place the caps on the center of the jars, then remove the bands from the water and tighten firmly, finger tight. You want exhaust air to be able to escape. Fill and cap all jars. If you have a jar lifter, use it to lower the jars carefully into the water bath so that each jar is completely submerged. Bring the water to a boil, and process according to the recipe.

Carefully remove the jars from the water and set them on a clean dish towel to cool. Wipe the water from the lids but try not to disturb the contents. As the jars cool, the lids will get sucked down, creating a seal. Some will pop, some will not, and you will be able to see if a jar has not sealed. Let the jars cool to room temperature and sit for 6 to 8 hours. They are now ready to store. If any jars fail to seal, reprocess or refrigerate.

Spring and Summer Pickled Vegetables

2 1/2 pounds green beans or asparagus
2 1/2 cups distilled white vinegar
2 cups water
1/4 cup sugar

6 large fresh dill sprigs
3/4 teaspoon red pepper flakes, divided
6 garlic cloves, peeled
6 (1/2-pint) jars

Trim the green beans or asparagus 1/4-inch shorter than the jars are tall. Bring the vinegar, water, and sugar to a boil. Stir until sugar has dissolved. Remove from heat. Remove the jars from the boiling water and place them on a hand towel on the counter. Add a sprig of the dill, 1/8 teaspoon red pepper flakes, and a small garlic clove into each of the 6 jars. Pack in the vegetables standing on their ends. Fill each jar with pickling brine 1/4-inch from the top,

then seal the jars with lids and rings. Carefully place the jars back into the hot water bath used to sterilize the jars. Simmer for 10 minutes. Remove the jars from the pot and place on a counter to cool. Check the lids for a tight fit by pressing on the center of the lid. If it pops, that means it's sealed. Let sit for two weeks in a cool, dark space. You can use any summer vegetable with this recipe and feel free to change up the seasonings.

continued »

Fall and Winter Pickled Vegetables

2 pounds mixed fall/winter vegetables
 (such as turnips, rutabaga, carrot
 varieties, kohlrabi, radishes, and beets)
6 cups apple cider vinegar
2 cups water
4 cups brown sugar
1/2 cup kosher salt

1 1/2-inch piece of fresh ginger,
 peeled and cut into coins
1/4 cup black peppercorns, toasted
8 whole cloves
2 star anise pods
2 (1-quart) jars or 4 (1-pint) jars

Preheat the oven to 400 degrees F. Cut the vegetables into sticks and set aside.

In a large saucepan over medium-high heat, bring the vinegar, water, brown sugar, salt, and ginger to a boil. Stir until the sugar is dissolved. Meanwhile, in a skillet or on a baking sheet, toast the spices until they become fragrant, about 2 minutes in a skillet or about 7 to 9 minutes in the oven. Remove from heat and add to the pickling brine. Allow to cool slightly. Place the vegetables in the jars, leaving 1/4-inch of space from the top, and pour the brine to cover. Cool overnight before using, or you can process in a hot water bath for extended shelf life.

Bread and Butter Pickles

12 cucumbers, washed and cut
 into 1/2-inch thick slices
2 cups julienned yellow onions
1/2 cup salt
4 cups sugar

4 cups apple cider vinegar
1 tablespoon yellow mustard seed
1/2 teaspoon turmeric
2 teaspoons celery seed

In a stainless-steel bowl, toss the cucumbers, onions, and salt. Cover completely with ice cubes and let sit for 3 hours.

In a heavy-bottom stockpot, combine the sugar, vinegar, mustard seed, turmeric, and celery seed. Bring to a boil, stirring constantly. Pour the cucumber and onion mixture into a colander and rinse with cold water. Drain well. Add the drained cucumbers and onions to the stockpot and bring to a boil again. Reduce the heat to medium and simmer for 5 minutes, stirring occasionally.

Remove the stockpot from the stove and pour the pickles into a storage container. Allow the pickles to cool at room temperature, then cover and refrigerate. The pickles will keep in the refrigerator for 3 to 4 weeks.

Toasted Spiced Pecans

We use Toasted Spiced Pecans in many different recipes at the restaurant: as crust for fish and chicken, in salads, or just for a tasty cocktail snack. Try fresh pecans in the fall when they are at the peak of the season.

2 tablespoons unsalted butter
1/8 teaspoon cayenne pepper
1/4 teaspoon salt

1/2 teaspoon sugar
1 cup pecan halves (about 1/2 pound)

Preheat the oven to 350 degrees F.

In a saucepan over medium heat, melt the butter, then stir in the cayenne pepper, salt, and sugar. Mix well. Add the pecans to the butter mixture, stirring continuously for 1 minute. Be mindful not to let the pecans burn.

On a baking sheet, spread out the pecans and bake for 4 minutes. They should be glossy and have a lightly toasted aroma, color, and flavor. Transfer the pecans to paper towels to absorb any excess oil. Once cooled to room temperature, store in an airtight container for up to 2 weeks.

Chicken Broth

Magnolias' Chicken Broth is used daily in the restaurant as the flavor base for many of our recipes. You will find Chicken Broth called for throughout this cookbook—in everything from soups to gravies. The preparation takes a little time, but once you've made the broth, it's easy to freeze and pull out when needed. Well worth the effort!

2 1/2 pounds chicken backs,
  rinsed with cold water
1 1/2 cups roughly chopped yellow onion
1 cup roughly chopped carrot
  (about 2 large carrots)
1 cup roughly chopped celery
  stalks, leaves removed

4 large garlic cloves, roughly chopped
2 bay leaves
8 fresh thyme sprigs or 1/2 teaspoon
  dried thyme
10 fresh parsley stems
6 cracked peppercorns
16 cups water

In a large stockpot over high heat, combine all the ingredients and bring them to a boil. Reduce to a simmer and slowly simmer, uncovered, for 2 1/2 hours, skimming off any foam and any excessive amounts of fat that appear on the top. Strain and discard the bones and vegetables.

Store broth in the refrigerator. It works best to store it in a clear container so you can see the protein sediment, which will gradually settle at the bottom. Once the broth has settled, pour the broth off slowly to keep the sediment separate from the clear broth. Discard any sediment. Once the broth has chilled, it is easy to remove the fat from the top by lifting it off with a spoon.

Store the finished broth in a covered container in the refrigerator for a few days or in the freezer for a few months.

Veal Stock

Veal can be intimidating, but this stock is very easy to make and allows for extra so that you can freeze some for next time. Just pour the leftovers into ice trays and freeze, then transfer to a resealable freezer bag. Pull out a cube or two when a recipe calls for some extra flavor.

5 pounds veal bones, cut into small pieces
Olive oil
6 ounces tomato paste
1 large yellow onion, roughly chopped
2 carrots, roughly chopped
3 stalks celery, roughly chopped, but with no leaves
1 leek, white portion only, well washed and roughly chopped

12 cups water
4 cups Chicken Broth (page 19)
2 bay leaves
6 cracked peppercorns
8 fresh thyme sprigs or ½ teaspoon dried thyme
10 fresh parsley stems
4 garlic cloves, roughly chopped

Preheat the oven to 500 degrees F.

Rub the veal bones with a little olive oil. Place the bones on a large baking sheet with raised sides and put it on the top shelf of the heated oven. Roast the bones for 30 to 35 minutes, or until a nice dark golden color is obtained. Remove the pan from the oven and reduce the heat to 450 degrees F. Using a rubber spatula or a wooden spoon, coat the bones with the tomato paste. Add the chopped onion, carrots, celery, and leek to the bones and return the pan to the oven. Continue to roast them for another 30 minutes.

Remove the bones and vegetables from the oven and transfer to a large stockpot. Take a little of the water and deglaze the baking sheet, scraping the bottom to get all the little bits of browned drippings and vegetables. Add the remaining water and the chicken broth, bay leaves, peppercorns, thyme, parsley, and garlic. If the water does not completely cover the bones, add enough to cover.

Slowly bring the stock to a boil, then reduce it to a simmer. It is important not to boil the stock because this will make it cloudy. Skim off any foam that appears on the top and any excess fat. Allow the stock to simmer for 4½ to 5 hours. It should be a rich golden brown. Strain, pressing the juice out of the vegetables.

Allow to cool and refrigerate until ready to use.

When the stock has been chilled, it is easy to remove the fat from it; the fat will rise to the top and you can lift it off with a spoon.

Store the finished broth in a covered container in the refrigerator for a few days or in the freezer for a few months.

Shrimp Stock

When peeling fresh raw shrimp, save your shrimp shells, wrap them in plastic, put them in the freezer, and pull them out as you need for stock. Shrimp stock can be used for all kinds of delicious dishes—shrimp bisque, shrimp pirloo, and as a base to make gumbos. Reduce it, add a little bit of butter and cream, and use it over some pasta or fish.

1/4 cup canola oil
1 medium-to-large onion, roughly chopped
1 rib celery, roughly chopped
1 carrot, peeled and roughly chopped
1 leek, white part only, roughly chopped
4 garlic cloves, crushed
3 fresh tarragon sprigs

6 fresh basil leaves
1 teaspoon black peppercorns
1 dried bay leaf
1 pound shrimp shells, crushed
1 (6-ounce) can tomato paste
1 cup brandy
8 cups water

In a large pot over medium heat, heat the canola oil. Add the onion, celery, carrot, leek, and garlic. Cook, stirring often, until soft but not brown, about 4 minutes. Add the tarragon, basil, black peppercorns, bay leaf, and crushed shrimp shells. Add the tomato paste and stir to coat the shells.

Continue to cook until the tomato paste has darkened a little, then deglaze the pan with the brandy and reduce the liquid by half, about 5 minutes. Add the water and bring to a simmer. Remove and discard any impurities that might have risen to the top. Simmer for 35 minutes. Strain and chill well, then transfer to pint containers and refrigerate for up to 1 week or freeze for up to 3 months.

Chicken Gravy

It's a universal truth that everything is better when served with gravy: meatloaf, fried chicken, country-fried steak, and mashed potatoes. This recipe can stand alone or enrich simple sauces. Adding pan drippings will spark flavor and deepen the color of this gravy if you happen to have some on hand.

4 tablespoons butter
1/2 cup flour
4 cups Chicken Broth (page 19), divided

2 tablespoons finely chopped fresh parsley
Salt
White pepper

In a heavy-bottom saucepan over low heat, melt the butter. Add the flour and stir until well combined, making a roux. Continue to cook over low heat for 5 minutes, stirring very frequently until the roux develops a light golden color and has a nutty aroma.

Increase the heat to medium and gradually add 2 cups of the chicken broth, stirring vigorously. Keep stirring constantly until the broth begins to thicken and is smooth. Gradually add the remaining 2 cups of broth, stirring constantly until the broth thickens into a gravy. Continue to simmer over low heat for 15 minutes to cook out the starchy flavor. Add the chopped parsley and any pan drippings. Season to taste with salt and white pepper.

Serve immediately.

Madeira Sauce

Madeira is a sweet, dry wine originally produced on the Madeira Island off the west coast of Africa. It was often served in Charleston homes during the nineteenth century. This is a labor-intensive reduction sauce, but it's delicious and well worth the effort. Any leftover sauce freezes well for the next time you need some.

1½ quarts Veal Stock (page 20)
1 tablespoon olive oil
1 cup roughly chopped yellow onion
1 tablespoon roughly chopped garlic
2 cups roughly chopped tomatoes
   (juice, seeds, and all)

¼ cup chopped fresh parsley stems
1 cup red wine
1 cup Madeira wine
Salt
White pepper

Pour the degreased veal stock into a saucepan and reduce by half over medium heat.

In a separate heavy-bottom saucepan, heat the oil. Add the onion, garlic, tomatoes, and parsley stems and sauté for 1 minute. Add the red wine and Madeira and bring the mixture to a boil. Reduce the heat to a simmer and allow the liquid to reduce by two-thirds.

Add the reduced veal stock to the vegetable mixture and continue to reduce by simmering. Reduce the liquid by one-third to approximately 2½ cups. As the liquid reduces, you will get a nice, dark color and intensified flavor. Strain the mixture, pressing the juices out of the vegetables, then strain again through a fine-mesh sieve. Return the sauce to the stove and reduce the volume by another third. Be sure to skim off any foam that may come to the top. At this point, you may strain once more through a cheesecloth or a very fine sieve.

Season with salt and white pepper to taste and a splash of Madeira if desired.

Note: It is important not to add any salt during the cooking process because the salt will concentrate as the liquids are reduced, resulting in an over-salted sauce.

Sweet-and-Hot Pork Shoulder and Rib Rub

MAKES ⅔ CUP

This rub is great to use for pork shoulder, beef brisket, and chicken. The cumin gives it a Southwestern feel and the cayenne some heat.

1 tablespoon plus 1 teaspoon granulated garlic powder

1 tablespoon plus 1 teaspoon granulated onion powder

2 tablespoons plus 1 teaspoon coarse sea salt

2 tablespoons plus 1 teaspoon freshly ground black pepper

2 teaspoons cumin

1 teaspoon cayenne pepper

3 tablespoons sugar

In a small bowl, combine all the ingredients. Rub generously onto the meat before cooking it. The seasoning can be stored in an airtight container or zip-top bag for up to 6 months.

Magnolias' Everyday Spicy Dry Rub

MAKES 4 TABLESPOONS

This versatile rub is a pantry staple and can be used on beef, pork, chicken, or fish. It's easily adjustable depending on your taste. For more heat, add ¼ teaspoon more of cayenne. For less heat, cut the cayenne in half. For a seafood dish, I recommend you switch out the cumin with ground coriander. You can take away half the salt and add in smoked sea salt for a smokier taste.

2 tablespoons granulated garlic powder

1 teaspoon cumin

3 teaspoons freshly ground black pepper

½ teaspoon cayenne pepper

2 teaspoons granulated onion powder

2½ teaspoons fine sea salt

In a small bowl, mix all of the seasonings together. Store in an airtight container or zip-top bag.

Magnolias' Blackening Spice

MAKES 1¼ CUPS

Blackening spice got its call to fame from Chef Paul Prudhomme, who was known for his Cajun and Creole specialties at the legendary K-Paul's in New Orleans. They actually had to put a halt on catching redfish for a few years due to the popularity of his blackened redfish dish. Magnolias' Blackening Spice is particularly good for fish dishes but can be used for chicken and pork as well.

Remember, dried spices lose their strength over time. Six months is about the max for freshness.

1 teaspoon freshly ground black pepper
½ teaspoon cayenne pepper
½ cup paprika
1 tablespoon chili powder
2 tablespoons granulated garlic powder
1 tablespoon granulated onion powder

1 tablespoon dried oregano
1 tablespoon dried basil
1 tablespoon dried thyme
1 tablespoon all-purpose flour
1 tablespoon cumin
1 tablespoon salt

In a small bowl, mix all of the ingredients together. Store in an airtight container or zip-top bag for up to 6 months.

Steak Marinade

MAKES ABOUT 1 CUP (ENOUGH FOR 4 TO 6 STEAKS)

This is a delicious marinade for all cuts of steak. My friend Darrell uses this marinade, fires up his steaks on the grill, and finishes them with a few pats of butter and Worcestershire sauce. Damn good!

¼ cup Worcestershire sauce
½ cup soy sauce
⅓ cup vegetable oil
2 tablespoons brown sugar

2 tablespoons finely chopped fresh chives
4 garlic cloves, minced
1½ teaspoons freshly ground black pepper
2 teaspoons balsamic vinegar

In a gallon-size zip-top bag, combine all the ingredients. Add the steaks and seal well.

Allow the steaks to marinate for 2 to 3 hours before cooking.

Herb Toast

This recipe creates a delicious toast that can be used with dips and salsa, or as a base for your favorite snack topping. Serve in whole slices or cut into triangles.

3/4 cup light olive oil
2 teaspoons mashed garlic
1 tablespoon very finely minced fresh chives
1 tablespoon very finely minced fresh basil

1/2 teaspoon salt
1/2 teaspoon freshly ground black pepper
1 long loaf of fresh, crusty French bread,
     cut into 1/4-inch-thick slices

Preheat the oven to 350 degrees F.

In a small bowl, combine the olive oil, garlic, chives, basil, salt, and pepper and allow to sit for 15 minutes. Place the slices of bread in a large bowl and drizzle on the oil and herb mixture while tossing the bread slices to coat.

Lay the bread slices out on a baking sheet and bake for 8 to 10 minutes, or until they are crisply toasted and light golden in color. Remove from the oven and allow them to cool to room temperature before serving or storing.

Buttermilk Biscuits

Homemade biscuits are deceptively simple, and every cook should have one in their repertoire. With a few subtle changes of ingredients, anything is possible! When I think about biscuits, they usually fall into one of seven different categories: buttermilk, cream, drop, rolled, scones, shortcake, and angel—they are all delicious! When we first put our Buttermilk Fried Chicken (page 153) on the menu, it was served with cream biscuits, but we now pair the dish with buttermilk biscuits. In a later chapter, I will tell you how to make one of the best shortcake biscuits you will ever have. Clearly, it's tough not to just ramble on when you talk about biscuits.

2 cups White Lily all-purpose
   flour, plus more for flouring
2 teaspoons Rumford baking powder*
1/4 teaspoon baking soda

1 teaspoon salt
1 stick (8 tablespoons) unsalted butter, frozen
3/4 cup buttermilk (do not use fat-
   free) plus 2 tablespoons, divided

Preheat the oven to 425 degrees F. Line a baking sheet with parchment paper or a baking mat.

In a large bowl, whisk together the flour, baking powder, baking soda, and salt. Using a box grater, grate the frozen butter into the flour mixture and continue to mix until it resembles coarse crumbs.

In the center of the mixture, make a well and pour 3/4 cup of cold buttermilk into the center, gently stirring until just combined.

Turn the dough onto a floured surface and pat into a rectangle (about 12 by 14 inches, 1/2-inch thick). Fold the rectangle into thirds, like folding a letter to put in an envelope. Turn dough 90 degrees and flatten it back into a rectangle, gathering up the dough crumbs. We are adding layers to the biscuits, similar to puff pastry. Repeat this process two more times, folding and pressing the dough for a total of three times. Don't kill it, just use light pressure. The more you touch the dough, the tougher it gets!

Roll the dough onto a floured surface about 1/2-inch thick. Use a 2- to 2 1/2-inch-round biscuit cutter to cut out the biscuits. Do not twist the cutter as you pierce the dough, just cut the dough with an up-and-down motion. Reroll any scraps and continue—you should have a total of 12 biscuits.

Transfer the biscuits to the prepared baking sheet. Press a small indent into the top of each biscuit with your thumb and brush the tops with the remaining buttermilk.

Bake until the biscuits are golden brown and flaky, about 15 minutes.

Note: The best baking powder to use in this recipe is aluminum-free baking powder, which contains no sodium aluminum sulfate, so it lacks the metallic taste. Rumford is a good brand of aluminum-free baking powder, found in most grocery stores.

White Lily Cream Biscuits

These are the lightest and easiest biscuits you'll ever make. Just mix the White Lily self-rising flour with the heavy cream. The butterfat in the heavy cream will do all the work—making you look impressive for fixing delicious homemade biscuits. Chopped herbs, spices, or cheese may be added to the dough for flavored biscuits.

2½ White Lily self–rising flour,
plus more for flouring

1½ cups heavy cream
3 tablespoons butter, melted

Preheat the oven to 400 degrees F.

In a mixing bowl, combine the flour and heavy cream. Stir with a spoon until it starts to come together and forms a wet sticky dough. Transfer the dough to a moderately floured surface. Lightly flour the top of the dough and then pat or roll it out to ½-inch thickness. Cut the biscuits using a 1-inch biscuit cutter, then place on an ungreased baking sheet and bake until golden brown, 8 to 10 minutes. Remove from the oven, brush with the melted butter, and serve immediately.

Cornbread

SERVES 4 TO 6

After much personal debate and taking into consideration that most people's preferred taste when it comes to cornbread is a little bit on the sweet side, this recipe is for y'all! We use cornbread in the restaurant for many of our dishes: fried for croutons, crumbled for seafood toppings, and used as the binder for the Crab and Yellow Corn Cakes (page 37) and Black-Eyed Pea Cakes (page 41). It's also delicious on its own with a little butter. The cast-iron skillet gives our cornbread a good crust.

1 seasoned, well-oiled 12-inch cast-iron skillet or a 9 x 13-inch baking pan
2 cups stone-ground yellow cornmeal
1 1/4 cups plus 2 tablespoons all-purpose flour
1 tablespoon plus 1 teaspoon Rumford baking powder*

1/2 teaspoon salt
1/2 cup sugar
4 eggs
2 cups buttermilk
5 tablespoons unsalted butter, melted
Canola oil, for oiling

Preheat the oven to 425 degrees F.

If using a cast-iron skillet, place the skillet in the preheated oven and allow the skillet to preheat, too. This helps make a golden-brown bottom crust.

In a large bowl, mix the cornmeal, flour, baking powder, salt, and sugar. In a separate bowl, lightly beat the eggs, then whisk in the buttermilk. Fold the buttermilk mixture into the dry mixture. Stir in the melted butter and mix well.

If you are using a cast-iron skillet, remove it from the oven. Rub the skillet or a baking pan with canola oil to lightly coat. Pour the batter into the baking dish.

Place the cornbread on the top shelf of the oven and bake for about 25 minutes, or until the top is brown and the center is firm. Insert a knife into the center to check for doneness. If it comes out clean, the cornbread is ready.

Allow the cornbread to rest in the skillet or pan for 8 to 10 minutes to cool slightly before cutting to serve.

*Note: The best baking powder to use in this recipe is aluminum-free baking powder, which contains no sodium aluminum sulfate, so it lacks the metallic taste. Rumford is a good brand of aluminum-free baking powder, found in most grocery stores.

Simple Pie Crust

Intimidated by making homemade pie crust? Don't be! This recipe will walk you through all the steps. A few pro tips: Chilling the pie crust dough between steps as indicated allows the gluten to relax and keeps the butter and shortening cold. This helps ensure a tender crust and keep the sides from shrinking and slipping down during baking. Patting out the dough into disks before placing them into the freezer helps when rolling out the dough for the pie tin.

12 tablespoons lightly salted butter, diced
4 tablespoons vegetable shortening
2 1/2 cups White Lily all-purpose
   flour, plus more for flouring

1/4 teaspoon salt
3 to 4 tablespoons ice water

Place the butter and the shortening on a plate and put in the freezer to firm the shortening and keep the butter cold while assembling the other ingredients.

In a large bowl, combine the flour and salt. Add the butter and shortening and cut into the flour by hand, in a mixer with a paddle, or in a food processor with a steel blade attached,

until the butter is completely incorporated with pieces no bigger than small peas. Slowly add the ice water, lightly combining the ingredients. It is important to add the water gradually. Mix until the dough is just combined and comes together to form a ball with a little molding by hand. Place on a lightly floured surface and pat the dough into a round, thin, flat disc, eliminating any creases and smoothing the edges. Wrap the disc in plastic wrap and refrigerate (or freeze) for at least an hour, or until firm.

On a lightly floured surface, roll out the dough into an approximately 14-inch circle that is $1/8$ to $3/16$ inch thick. Give the dough quarter turns as you are rolling it so that the thickness remains uniform. Brush off any excess flour.

Roll the dough over your rolling pin and lay it into a pie tin. Trim the excess dough, leaving an overhang of about 1 inch. Fold the overhang inward to rest on the rim of the pie tin. Pat the crust to fit the tin and crimp the edges of the crust using two fingers and a thumb. Refrigerate for 30 minutes or up to 1 day.

When ready to bake, fill the pie shell with the desired filling and bake at its required temperature and time until the crust is golden and the filling is cooked, 35 to 40 minutes.

Note: If using just as a baked shell, bake the pie shell alone for 15 to 20 minutes at 425 degrees F until it is golden all over, rotating it a quarter turn once or twice through the baking process.

APPETIZERS

Crab and Yellow Corn Cakes with Tomato, Corn, and Chive Butter

MAKES 8 (3-OUNCE) CAKES

Crab has always been a delicacy. Today, it's become very expensive and good-quality crab meat is getting harder to find. There are only a handful of local pickers on the East Coast and only two that I know of on the Gulf. I bet 90 percent of the crab meat in the grocery store comes from outside of the United States.

Fresh crab meat is available as colossal, jumbo lump, lump, backfin, and claw. Most Southerners prefer jumbo lump crab, so this is what we serve. My personal preference is claw meat. It's a working muscle with a sweeter taste—and it's a lot less expensive. Claw meat does take more work to remove from the shell, but it's worth the effort if you're just making a small batch.

All crab meat should be picked over to remove any remaining shell. Once you open the container, use the lid and press lightly on the crab meat to drain off any excess liquid. Spread the crab out on a plate or baking sheet and check closely for shells. Try your best not to break up the lumps.

1/3 cup finely minced red onion
1/3 cup finely minced red bell pepper
1/3 cup fresh corn, cut off the cob
1 tablespoon minced fresh tarragon
1/3 cup Duke's mayonnaise
1 pound jumbo lump crab or
   lump crab, well picked

3/4 to 1 cup Cornbread crumbs (page 33)
2 teaspoons kosher salt
1/4 teaspoon white pepper
1/8 teaspoon cayenne pepper
6 tablespoons light olive oil, divided
Tomato, Corn, and Chive Butter (page 38)

In a mixing bowl, combine the onion, bell pepper, corn, tarragon, and mayonnaise. Gently fold in the crab meat. Add the cornbread crumbs, white pepper, and cayenne pepper. Let the mixture rest for 5 minutes. The cornbread will absorb some of the moisture and the mixture will stay together. Divide the crab batter into 8 equal balls. Form each ball into a puck-shaped patty and place on a baking sheet. Refrigerate for 30 minutes.

Preheat the oven to 375 degrees F.

In a large, heavy-bottom frying pan with a lid, heat 3 tablespoons of olive oil over medium-high heat until it shimmers. Carefully place four crab cakes in the pan and sear for 3 to 4 minutes, or until golden brown. I recommend frying them covered since the corn in the cakes will pop in the hot oil. Gently turn the cakes over and sear on the other side for 2 to 3 minutes or until golden brown. Transfer them to a baking sheet. Wipe out the pan, pour in the remaining 3 tablespoons of oil, and repeat the cooking process with the other four crab cakes. When finished, add the remaining crab cakes to the baking sheet and place in the oven. Warm thoroughly for about 5 minutes. Serve with tomato, corn, and chive butter.

continued »

Tomato, Corn, and Chive Butter

MAKES 2 CUPS

13 tablespoons unsalted butter, divided
2 tablespoons finely minced yellow onion
1 teaspoon finely minced garlic
1/4 cup dry vermouth
1 cup Chicken Broth (page 19)
2 tablespoons heavy cream

1/2 cup peeled, seeded, and finely
   chopped fresh tomato, divided
1 cup cooked fresh yellow corn kernels
Salt
1/4 cup chopped fresh chives

In a heavy-bottom sauté pan over medium heat, melt 1 tablespoon of butter. Sauté the onion and garlic for 2 to 3 minutes or until the onion is translucent. Turn the heat up to medium-high and add the vermouth. Cook, stirring occasionally, until the vermouth is reduced by half.

Add the chicken broth and reduce the liquid by two-thirds. Add the heavy cream and continue to reduce the liquid until it thickens and becomes very bubbly. Add 1 tablespoon of the chopped tomato and all the corn. Reduce the heat to low and add the remaining 12 tablespoons of butter, one tablespoon at a time, stirring constantly. Allow each tablespoon to melt before adding the next tablespoon of butter. While adding the butter, try to keep the temperature between 130 and 150 degrees F. It is very important that the sauce does not boil, or the butter will separate. The butter will also separate if the sauce becomes too cool.

After the butter is incorporated, fold in the remainder of the chopped tomatoes. Season with salt to taste. Add the chives and serve immediately or hold in a warm area, such as on top of the stove but off the burner, for 30 to 40 minutes. Do not put the chives in until it is time to serve the sauce, because their color will fade.

Black-Eyed Pea Cakes

MAKES 24 (2-OUNCE) OR 16 (3-OUNCE) CAKES

My first experience with trying to make Black-Eyed Pea Cakes was in Hawaii. My wife, Martha, and I lived out on the North Shore near a big surf break known as "Pipeline." Our house was a couple of miles outside of a small town called Haleiwa. We lived right in back of a famous surfer named Gerry Lopez.

Martha and I had just relocated from Australia, and it was our first New Year's back in the States after getting married. My father-in-law, from the great state of Alabama, has a family tradition of eating "peace and plenty"—collard greens, black-eyed peas, and cornbread—for the New Year's Day meal.

I wanted to fix this traditional meal and quickly learned it's not so easy to find these staples outside of the Southern states, especially in small-town Hawaii. I checked everywhere! Finally, I ran into a local guy whose family ran Matsumoto, a shaved-ice place that had been there since the 1950s. I saw they had a few different toppings (for the cones) that had beans. When I asked about the black-eyed peas, he started laughing. "Collard greens? Black-eyed peas? Where you from, bro?" He told me to run into town and check some of the Indian grocery stores. Lo and behold, I found some peas that came pretty close. My first attempt, I mixed all three—the can of black-eyed peas, canned chopped greens, and Jiffy cornbread mix to hold it all together. The result was more like a falafel. That early experiment has evolved into Magnolias' Black-Eyed Pea Cakes, which are served with a Tomato Salsa in the summer and what's now called "Comeback Sauce" in the winter months. We use dried peas that we soak, but if you're short on time, canned black-eyed peas work fine.

2 cups dried black-eyed peas,
  rinsed with cold water
6 cups water
3 chicken bouillon cubes
3 teaspoons salt, divided
1 smoked pork neck bone
1 cup plus 2 tablespoons olive oil, divided
1/2 cup minced yellow onion
1/2 cup minced green onion
1/2 cup minced red onion
2 tablespoons minced garlic
1/4 cup chopped red pepper

1 tablespoon stemmed, seeded,
  and minced jalapeño
2 tablespoons minced fresh cilantro
1 tablespoon cumin
Dash cayenne pepper
1 teaspoon freshly ground black pepper
2 cups fresh Cornbread crumbs (page 33)
2 cups stone-ground yellow cornmeal
Red and Yellow Tomato Salsa
  (optional, page 43)
Comeback Sauce (optional, page 43)

In a large, heavy-bottom saucepan, combine the peas, water, bouillon cubes, 1 teaspoon of salt, and the smoked neck bone. Bring to a boil. Reduce to a simmer and cook for 55 minutes or until the peas are very soft and their skins have broken. Add additional water if needed, 1 cup at a time; peas should be slightly covered with liquid while simmering. Remove the neck bone and strain.

continued »

In a sauté pan, heat 2 tablespoons of olive oil until very hot. Quickly sauté the yellow onion, green onion, red onion, garlic, red pepper, jalapeño, and cilantro until just tender, 2 to 3 minutes. Add the cumin, cayenne pepper, remaining 2 teaspoons of salt, and the black pepper. Mix well. Transfer the mixture to a plate and let cool.

Next, mash the beans with a mixer with a flat paddle beater, a potato masher, or with your hands until the beans are creamed. Most of the beans will be broken and their mashed starches will come together to bond the cakes. Add the vegetable mixture and mix well. Add the cornbread crumbs and mix well. Adjust seasonings as needed.

Using a ¼ measuring cup, scoop the mixture and form into balls to make the cakes. Lightly press them down to make them about ½ inch thick. Dust lightly with cornmeal.

In a heavy-bottom skillet over medium heat, add 2 to 3 tablespoons of olive oil per batch. Depending on the size of your skillet, add the cakes and cook on each side for 2 to 3 minutes, or until golden brown. While cooking the cakes in batches, the cakes can be held in a 250-degree F oven until cooking is complete.

Serve with red and yellow tomato salsa or comeback sauce, if desired.

Note: The cakes can be made ahead of time and refrigerated. However, be sure to bring them to room temperature before cooking.

Red and Yellow Tomato Salsa

MAKES 2 CUPS

1 medium red tomato, seeded and diced
1 medium yellow tomato, seeded and diced
1 garlic clove, minced
1 small jalapeño, stemmed,
   seeded and minced
1 green onion, thinly sliced

$1/4$ cup chopped fresh cilantro
$1/4$ cup diced red onion
2 tablespoons fresh lime juice
1 teaspoon red wine vinegar
Salt
Pepper

In a small bowl, combine all the ingredients except salt and pepper. Sprinkle lightly with salt and pepper and let sit for a couple of minutes. Add more salt and pepper to taste if needed.

Comeback Sauce

MAKES 1 $1/2$ CUPS

It's widely held that Comeback sauce originated in Jackson, Mississippi, but after that, there's a little disagreement over the details. Some say it was from the Mayflower Café. Others will say the Rotisserie back in the early 1930s. Most locals agree it was served by the Greek restaurants in town in the 1970s and '80s— first as a salad dressing and later a sauce. Our version is a combination of a Greek dressing and a rémoulade sauce. After you try this recipe, you can almost figure out the dipping sauce served by some of the leading fast-food chicken restaurants. (Maybe add a little smoked paprika.)

1 cup Duke's mayonnaise
$1/4$ cup chili sauce
2 tablespoons ketchup
2 teaspoons Worcestershire sauce
1 teaspoon lemon juice
$1/2$ teaspoon paprika

1 garlic clove, finely minced
2 tablespoons minced yellow onion
Hot sauce
Salt
Freshly ground black pepper

In a small bowl or food processor, combine all the ingredients and mix well. Store in the refrigerator in an airtight container for up to 7 days.

Down South Egg Rolls with Red Pepper Purée, Spicy Mustard, and Peach Chutney

MAKES 8 EGG ROLLS

This dish began as a random special one night and soon became one of Magnolias' signature appetizers. It was popular with diners and an instant hit with the press as an early example of "fusion cuisine," merging Southern ingredients with a traditional Asian preparation. With a couple of small changes over the years, the Down South Egg Roll is still on our menu and remains a customer favorite.

2 tablespoons light olive oil
2 cups julienned yellow onion
1 tablespoon plus 1 teaspoon minced garlic
1 pound boneless, skinless chicken thighs, cut into thin strips, removing all fat
1 cup small strips tasso ham
2 packed cups Magnolias' Collard Greens, chopped and well-drained (page 181)

8 egg roll wrappers
1 cup plus 2 tablespoons cornstarch, divided, plus more for dusting
2 teaspoons cold water
12 cups peanut oil or canola oil for frying
Red Pepper Purée (page 46)
Spicy Mustard (page 47)
Peach Chutney (page 47)

In a large, heavy-bottom frying pan over medium heat, heat the olive oil. Add the onion, garlic, chicken, and tasso ham. Sauté, stirring constantly, for 5 minutes, or until the chicken is fully cooked. Squeeze all juice from the collard greens and add them to the frying pan. Cook for 1 to 2 minutes to heat the collards and meld all of the flavors. Remove from the heat and pour the mixture into a colander to drain. Spread the mixture out onto a baking sheet and let cool; squeeze out as much moisture as you can. You can easily do this by squeezing the mixture in a clean tea towel, in batches if necessary. The drier, the better.

On a clean, dry surface dusted lightly with cornstarch, lay out the egg roll wrappers and set them up in a diamond pattern, with the bottom points facing you. Portion ¾ cup of filling on the centers of each of the 8 wrappers.

Put 2 tablespoons of cornstarch in a small bowl and slowly add the cold water, stirring until you have a smooth, lump-free paste. Lightly brush the edges of each egg roll wrapper with the cornstarch mixture. Fold the bottom quarter of the diamond up toward the top. Fold the two sides inward to form an envelope. Bring the top corner down toward you. Gently press the edges to seal the rolls. Lightly dust the egg rolls with the remaining 1 cup cornstarch, as needed, to keep them dry.

In a deep fryer or deep-frying pan, pour the peanut oil. If you are using something smaller, use only enough oil to fill the fryer about three-quarters of the way up the sides. Gradually heat the oil to 340 degrees F by starting the heat on medium and slowly increasing the heat to medium-high. Never put oil in any frying container and turn the heat on high.

continued »

Once the oil is heated, add 4 egg rolls. (Adding too many egg rolls to the oil will bring down the temperature of the oil. Try to keep the temperature as close to a consistent 340 degrees F as possible.) Continue to cook the egg rolls, turning frequently, until they are golden brown and crispy. Initially, try to keep the egg rolls submerged. As they brown, they will float to the top. If the oil is too hot, the egg roll skins will brown before the egg rolls heat throughout. Remove the egg rolls from the oil and transfer them to paper towels to absorb any excess oil. Repeat the process for the remaining 4 egg rolls.

Immediately serve with red pepper purée, spicy mustard, and chutney. For 8 egg rolls, you will need 1 1/2 cups of each accompaniment. At the restaurant, we spread a dollop of the purée and mustard on the base of the plate, halve the egg roll on a bias, and top with chutney.

Red Pepper Purée

MAKES 3 1/2 CUPS

2 tablespoons plus 1 teaspoon olive oil
1/2 cup roughly chopped yellow onion
1 teaspoon roughly chopped garlic
1/4 cup all-purpose flour
2 1/2 cups Chicken Broth (page 19), divided

1 1/2 cups chopped flesh from 3 large
   roasted red peppers, or 3 (4-ounce)
   jars pimientos, drained and chopped
1/4 cup chopped fresh basil
Salt
Cayenne pepper

In a heavy-bottom saucepan over medium heat, heat the olive oil. Add the chopped onion and garlic and sauté for 1 minute. Reduce the heat and make a roux by adding the flour and stirring until well combined. Continue to cook over low heat for 2 minutes, stirring constantly. Do not let the onions or flour brown. Increase the heat to medium and add 1 1/4 cups of the chicken broth, stirring vigorously. Keep stirring vigorously until the broth thickens and is smooth. Gradually add the remaining 1 1/4 cups of chicken broth, the red pepper, and the basil, stirring constantly until the broth thickens into a sauce.

Bring the sauce to a low boil, then simmer over medium heat for 10 minutes to cook out the starchy flavor. Skim off any skin that may come to the top. Remove the sauce from the stove and let it cool, stirring occasionally, for 10 minutes. Transfer the mixture to a food processor or blender and purée until smooth. Season to taste with salt and cayenne pepper. Use at once or pour into a storage container and refrigerate for up to one week.

Spicy Mustard

MAKES 1 1/2 CUPS

1 tablespoon olive oil
1/2 cup roughly chopped yellow onion
1/2 cup roughly chopped unpeeled gingerroot
1 teaspoon chopped garlic
1 stemmed and chopped jalapeño

1/2 lemon
1/2 orange
1/2 cup soy sauce
6 ounces cold water
1 cup Colman's dry mustard

In a heavy-bottom saucepan over medium heat, heat the olive oil until hot. Add the onion, ginger, garlic, and jalapeño. Sauté for 2 minutes. Quarter the lemon and orange and squeeze the juice over the vegetables. Rough chop the rinds and add them. Add the soy sauce. Cook for 5 minutes over medium heat. Strain and press out the juices into a medium bowl. Discard the solids.

In a small mixing bowl, slowly add the cold water to the dry mustard, stirring until you have a smooth, lump-free paste. Let this mixture sit for 10 minutes, then stir it into the soy mixture. Use at once or transfer the mixture to a storage container, let cool at room temperature, cover, and refrigerate for up to 3 weeks.

Peach Chutney

MAKES 2 1/2 CUPS

2 cups peeled fresh or frozen peaches
1/2 cup minced yellow onion
1 tablespoons plus 1 teaspoon peeled and finely minced ginger

1/2 cup finely diced red pepper
1/2 cup light brown sugar
1/2 cup granulated sugar
2 tablespoons apple cider vinegar

In a heavy-bottom saucepan over medium heat, combine all of the ingredients and stir well. Bring to a boil, stirring constantly, then simmer for 25 to 30 minutes, until the chutney begins to thicken slightly and is syrupy. Remove from the heat and allow the chutney to cool. Use at once or transfer to a storage container and refrigerate for up to 3 weeks.

Note: If using fresh peaches, select fairly firm ones that are just beginning to ripen. Fully ripened fruit will break down in the cooking process.

Pimiento Cheese

Magnolias' Pimiento Cheese, or "Southern Caviar," as we call it, has been featured across many media channels, including Food Network's Best Thing I Ever Ate, *several big-city newspaper food sections, and now on TikTok and Snapchat. Who would have thought that a simple Southern staple would become a national sensation?*

For this recipe, I recommend using fresh roasted red peppers instead of the canned ones, as they produce a much better flavor. If you like more heat in your pimiento cheese, try adding 1 tablespoon of finely minced jalapeños and a dash of your favorite hot sauce.

5 large Roasted Red Peppers (recipe
    follows), chopped, or 2½ cups
    jarred, diced red pimientos
1 cup stuffed green olives, finely chopped
1¼ pounds New York or Vermont sharp
    white cheddar cheese, grated

¼ cup freshly grated Parmesan cheese
¼ cup Duke's mayonnaise
1 tablespoon chopped fresh parsley
½ teaspoon freshly ground black pepper
Cayenne pepper

Combine all the ingredients except the cayenne pepper in a mixing bowl and mix well. Season to taste with cayenne pepper. Cover and refrigerate until ready to serve.

Roasted Red Peppers

Be sure to use healthy-looking peppers with good, thick flesh. If using thin peppers, the roasting time will be shorter.

5 large red peppers

Olive oil

Preheat the oven to 500 degrees F.

Wash and dry the peppers. Rub the peppers with olive oil to lightly coat them. Place the peppers on a baking sheet and roast them on the top shelf of the oven for about 25 minutes, turning once or twice. The skin should be well-blistered and blackened in some places.

Remove the peppers from the oven. Place them in a small bowl and cover tightly with plastic wrap. Let the peppers cool for 10 to 15 minutes. The skin will become loose and very easy to remove.

Peel the skin off of the peppers. Remove the stems, cores, and seeds; do not rinse.

Note: At this point you may use the peppers in any manner that you would use jarred pimientos.

Warm Pimiento Cheese and Crab Dip

MAKES 3 1/2 CUPS

This recipe was created as a dish to serve at a Preservation Society of Charleston book-signing party for our first cookbook, Magnolias Southern Cuisine. *The flavors come together really well. It's a great appetizer or "covered dish" to bring to a party as the dip reheats easily. Serve with Herb Toast (page 28) or your favorite crackers.*

Crab Dip (recipe follows)
1 1/2 cups Pimiento Cheese (page 49)

1 tablespoon very finely minced
  fresh basil, for garnish
Herb Toast (page 28)

In a medium saucepan over medium heat, heat the crab dip, then fold in the pimiento cheese. Stir gently until the cheese has fully melted into the crab dip. Transfer to a bowl and garnish with basil. Serve warm with the toast or your favorite crackers or dipping chips.

Crab Dip

MAKES 2 CUPS

1 tablespoon butter
1 cup finely minced yellow onion
1 tablespoon finely minced garlic
2 tablespoons heavy cream
8 ounces cream cheese, cubed
  and room temperature
1 pound lump crab meat, gently picked
  over for shell and drained of any liquid

1 teaspoon chopped fresh parsley
1 teaspoon chopped fresh basil
1 teaspoon chopped fresh chives
Dash salt
Dash freshly ground black pepper
Dash cayenne pepper
Herb Toast (page 28)

In a heavy-bottom saucepan over medium heat, melt the butter. Add the onion and garlic and sauté for 2 minutes, stirring to prevent browning. Add the cream and stir to combine. Add the cream cheese and whisk until melted and the mixture is smooth.

Remove the saucepan from the heat. Transfer the mixture to a bowl and allow to cool for 10 minutes at room temperature. Fold in the crab meat, herbs, and seasonings. Serve immediately or refrigerate and serve chilled. Accompany with the toast or your favorite cracker.

Cornmeal Fried Oysters

SERVES 4 TO 6

The old Lowcountry rule of thumb is months that end in R are oyster-eating times. During the fall and winter months, I put fried oysters back on the menu at the first sign of cold water. When making this dish, I suggest you grab a couple of pints of your favorite local oysters—the briny flavor is better. If local oysters are not available, you might add a tablespoon or two of buttermilk and a dash of hot sauce to your raw oysters before breading.

A couple of pointers: Just cook one or two oysters to start to make sure you have the seasoning right, and don't try to fry too many oysters at once.

½ gallon peanut oil or canola oil, for frying
1 pint oysters, drained
Cornmeal Breading (recipe follows)

Salt
Jalapeño–Lime Aioli (recipe
  follows), for serving

Preheat the oil to 350 degrees F in a large skillet or deep fryer.

Place half of the oysters in the breading and toss them to coat well. Allow them to rest in the breading for 1 minute or so. Remove from the breading and shake off the excess. Fry the oysters until they are crispy and light golden brown in color, about 2 minutes. Transfer to paper towels to cool. Repeat these steps for the remaining oysters. Season more with salt if desired. Serve with jalapeño-lime aioli.

Cornmeal Breading

MAKES APPROXIMATELY 1¾ CUPS

¾ cup all-purpose flour
¾ cup cornmeal
⅓ cup cornstarch

¾ teaspoon fine sea salt
¾ teaspoon white pepper
¼ teaspoon freshly ground black pepper

Sift the ingredients together. Reserve.

Jalapeño-Lime Aioli

MAKES ½ CUP

1 tablespoon roughly chopped
  jalapeño, seeds and all
½ cup Duke's mayonnaise

1 tablespoon fresh lime juice
1 tablespoon chopped fresh parsley
¼ teaspoon fine sea salt

In a food processor with a steel blade, combine all of the ingredients. Process until the jalapeño and the parsley are puréed. Use immediately, or cover and refrigerate for up to 3 days.

Roasted Oysters with Country Ham Cracklings

MAKES 24 OYSTERS

There are hundreds of oyster roasts held each weekend during fall and winter months in the Lowcountry. Some oysters are simply steamed in a wet burlap bag and served with cocktail sauce and melted butter. Others are a bit more refined: roasted or grilled with different toppings and assorted butters. Either way, you're bound to have fun gathering around a fire to eat these briny delicacies. This recipe is an elegant way to prepare freshly shucked local oysters.

6 tablespoons freshly grated
   Parmesan cheese, divided
1 cup Duke's mayonnaise
1 teaspoon Worcestershire sauce

24 local oysters, top shell removed,
   bottom muscle cut, and shell wiped
   clean of shell pieces and mud
3/4 cup Country Ham Cracklings (recipe follows)
1 lemon, cut into 8 wedges, for serving

Preheat the oven to 400 degrees F.

In a small bowl, mix 3 tablespoons of the Parmesan cheese with the mayonnaise and Worcestershire sauce.

Drain most of the liquor (liquid) off of the oysters, then spoon about 1 teaspoon of the mayo mixture over the oyster on the half shell. Using a flat knife, spread the topping around the oyster. Sprinkle the oysters with the ham cracklings and the remaining 3 tablespoons of Parmesan cheese.

Transfer the oysters to a baking sheet and place on the upper shelf of the oven. Roast the oysters for 8 to 10 minutes, or until the oysters are bubbly and lightly browned. Remove from the oven and allow the oysters to cool for 1 to 2 minutes. Serve with lemon wedges.

Country Ham Cracklings

MAKES 1 CUP

1/2 pound country ham trimmings

3 tablespoons light olive oil

Chop the ham trimmings finely by hand or pulse them in batches in a food processor into small pieces. For best results, freeze the ham first and chop when frozen. (Because of the curing process, the ham never freezes rock hard.)

Put the ham and oil in a heavy-bottom pan and bring the heat gradually up to medium, cooking the trimmings slowly to render the ham of most of its fat. Cook the trimmings for 15 to 20 minutes, stirring frequently, or until the ham begins to become somewhat caramelized and is crispy. Once you hear it sizzle and crackle, remove the pan from the heat and, using a slotted spoon, move the cracklings onto paper towels to drain and cool. Use immediately or cool to room temperature, transfer to a storage container, cover, and refrigerate.

Spicy Steamed Peel-and-Eat Shrimp

SERVES 8 TO 10

Peel-and-eat shrimp is another Southern classic that brings people together.

The cocktail sauce for this recipe is not your standard ketchup-and-horseradish cocktail sauce. The mirin and rice vinegar add an acidic kick that's great on both peel-and-eat and fried shrimp.

I am not really sure where the sauce originated, but the first time I ever had it was when I was a child visiting my grandmother in St. Augustine, Florida. There was a restaurant named Colley's right near the Bridge of Lions. It was open for years and featured all-you-can-eat fried shrimp. My first time eating fried shrimp, I didn't know that you weren't supposed to eat the shells. My grandmother looked over and asked, "What did you do with the tails?" This spot closed many years ago, but Pomare's opened a spot called Osteen's right across the street, and they still serve the same style butterflied fried shrimp. Lonnie and his family have been running the place now for about forty years. They don't take reservations and it's packed every night. You have to get there early and just grab a seat on the red benches outside.

continued »

Water, beer (cook's preference), or a combination of both, ½-inch deep in a large pot
3 pounds large fresh shrimp

⅓ cup local seafood spice blend or Old Bay Seasoning, plus more for serving (optional)
¼ cup salted butter, melted
Cocktail Sauce (recipe follows)

In a large pot over high heat, add the liquid and heat until steaming. Sprinkle the shrimp with the seasoning and place them in a steamer basket in the pot. Cover and allow the shrimp to steam for 4 to 6 minutes with an occasional stir. They should be nice and pink, without any translucent, raw-looking areas. Remove the shrimp from the heat and allow them to cool for a few minutes. Transfer to a serving dish and serve with the melted butter, cocktail sauce, and additional spice blend, if desired.

Note: If you do not have a steamer basket, you can boil the shrimp using the same ingredients. Season the liquid with the spice blend and bring the liquid to a rapid boil. Add the shrimp and cook uncovered for 4 to 6 minutes, or until the shrimp are pink, without any translucent, raw-looking areas.

Cocktail Sauce

MAKES 1 ½ CUPS

1 cup Duke's mayonnaise
1 tablespoon ketchup
1 tablespoon melted butter
1 tablespoon mirin
2 teaspoons rice vinegar
¼ teaspoon paprika

¼ teaspoon garlic powder
¾ teaspoon onion powder
1 tablespoon granulated sugar
Hot sauce (optional)
1 to 2 tablespoons water, as needed

In a small mixing bowl, combine the mayonnaise, ketchup, butter, mirin, rice vinegar, spices, and sugar. Add hot sauce, if desired. Pour in the water a little at a time to reach the desired thickness. Cover and refrigerate for a couple hours before serving. This will keep in the refrigerator in an airtight container for 1 week.

Fried Green Tomatoes

Several years ago, Magnolias was named one of the places to visit in the book 1,000 Places to See Before You Die. *The author had visited the restaurant and was particularly taken by our signature fried green tomatoes. It's a stack of delicious sweet-and-salty flavors and is likely the number-one appetizer on our menu today. We cook up to five hundred orders a week!*

3 cups all-purpose flour, seasoned
   with salt and pepper to taste
3 cups buttermilk
3 eggs
2 cups panko breadcrumbs
3/4 cup yellow cornmeal
1/3 cup julienned fresh basil
18 (1/4-inch-thick) slices of green tomatoes
   (approximately 5 whole tomatoes)

4 cups canola oil
6 (1 1/2 ounces) slices country ham, halved
Caramelized Onion and White
   Cheddar Grits (page 58)
Tomato Chutney (page 58)
Tomato Butter (page 58)

This is a standard breading procedure that can be used for frying many kinds of vegetables. You'll need 3 separate containers, or use 3 large freezer bags to save time on cleanup.

Put the seasoned flour in the first container. In the second, mix the buttermilk and eggs together. In the third, mix the panko, cornmeal, and basil. Evenly coat all tomatoes in the seasoned flour, shaking off the excess. Dunk in the buttermilk mixture, and shake off any excess. Dredge the tomatoes in the final container of panko-cornmeal mixture, making sure to coat them well. (Tip: Use one hand for the dry step and the other for the wet steps. This will help keep the batter on the tomatoes and not your hands.)

In a large skillet or deep fryer, heat the canola oil to 325 degrees F. Fry the tomatoes in small batches until golden brown, about 3 to 4 minutes per side. Transfer to paper towels to drain and keep warm. Sear the ham in a sauté pan. Place 6 appetizer-size plates on the counter. In the center of each plate, place a 3-ounce scoop of grits. Starting with a single slice of fried green tomato, top the grits with alternating slices of tomato and ham (there should be 1 1/2 ounces or 2 thin slices of ham per person). Finish the stack with a slice of tomato. Crown the stack with a spoonful of the tomato chutney. Finish the dish using a 2-ounce ladle to drizzle the tomato butter around the edge of the plate.

continued »

Caramelized Onion and White Cheddar Grits

SERVES 6

3 cups water
1 cup stone–ground grits
1/2 cup heavy cream
1 small onion, julienned and caramelized
  (see Caramelized Onions, page 61)

1 cup grated white cheddar cheese
Coarse sea salt
Freshly ground black pepper

In a heavy-bottom pot, bring the water to a boil. Slowly pour in the grits and stir continuously for the first 5 minutes to prevent lumps. Turn the heat down to low and simmer for 30 minutes, stirring occasionally. Add the heavy cream and cook for 15 minutes more.

The grits should be thick and plump; add more water or heavy cream if needed. Stir in the caramelized onion and white cheddar cheese. Cook for 5 minutes more. Season to taste with salt and pepper. Keep warm until ready to serve.

Tomato Chutney

MAKES 1 PINT

4 cups sugar
2 cups apple cider vinegar
6 cups julienned tomatoes, drained

2 cups julienned yellow onions
1 jalapeño, minced
2 teaspoons red pepper flakes

In a heavy-bottom saucepan over medium-high heat, bring the sugar and vinegar to a boil. Reduce the heat to a simmer and reduce the volume by half. Add the tomatoes, onions,

jalapeño, and red pepper flakes and cook for about 1 hour, until the mixture becomes syrupy. After it cooks down, remove from the heat and cool. It will thicken as it cools.

Tomato Butter

MAKES 1 CUP

1 tablespoon olive oil
3 shallots, minced
1 cup tomato juice
1/4 cup heavy (whipping) cream

3/4 pound (3 sticks) unsalted
  butter, cut into small pieces
1/2 teaspoon salt
Pinch white pepper

In a heavy-bottom saucepan over medium-high heat, warm the olive oil. Add the shallots and sauté until translucent. Add the tomato juice and reduce until it becomes bubbly and thick. Add the cream and reduce until thickened,

stirring often. Turn the heat down and, stirring constantly, add the butter a little bit at a time, until all is incorporated. Season with salt and white pepper. Remove from the heat and hold in a warm area until ready to serve.

Panfried Chicken Livers

Chicken livers—you either love them or not. I'm a big fan. We panfry ours in seasoned flour with hot oil just covering them. They release moisture into the oil and sometimes splatter, so make sure to use a screen or lid to cover the livers when cooking. The best way to eat this dish is by having a small amount of caramelized onions, country ham, and liver on your fork, running it through the rich Madeira sauce. Some people say this is the best chicken liver dish in the South!

Caramelized Onions (recipe follows)
1 pound chicken livers
1/2 cup all-purpose flour
1 teaspoon salt
1 teaspoon freshly ground black pepper

2 tablespoons light olive oil,
   plus more as needed
6 ounces country ham, sliced very thin
1 pint Madeira Sauce (page 23)

Prepare the caramelized onions. Set aside.

Preheat the oven to 350 degrees F.

Trim any fat or sinew from the chicken livers. In a bowl, combine the flour, salt, and pepper, mixing well. Dust the livers with the flour mixture, making sure to cover them completely. Shake off excess flour so that it does not burn the pan.

In a heavy-bottom frying pan over medium-high heat, pour in the olive oil. Gently place the livers in the hot oil. Be careful—they will spit and splatter the oil, so cover the pan with a lid or splatter guard. Sauté on one side for 1 to 2 minutes, or until golden brown. Uncover the pan, flip the livers over, and continue to cook.

If all the oil has been absorbed, add a little more, 1 teaspoon at a time.

Remove from the stovetop and place the pan in the oven for 3 to 4 minutes, or until the livers are firm and cooked through. While the livers are cooking, sauté the ham in a heavy-bottom frying pan over medium heat until the ham edges curl up. Add the caramelized onions to the frying pan with the ham and heat.

When ready to serve, remove the livers from the oven. Divide the livers and ham among 4 plates. Mound the onions in the center of each plate. Spoon the Madeira sauce around the ham, liver, and onions. Serve immediately.

Caramelized Onions

MAKES 1 CUP

1 tablespoon olive oil, plus more as needed

2 cups thinly sliced yellow onions,
   cut in 1/4-inch ringed slices

In a heavy-bottom frying pan over high heat, heat the olive oil until smoking. Lay the onion slices in the hot oil. Keep the slices intact and do not loosen them into rings until after the initial searing. Cook for 1 to 2 minutes without turning to start the caramelization process. Continue to cook, tossing occasionally, until the onions caramelize and turn golden brown.

At this point, the slices may break into rings. Watch the heat and reduce it slightly if it appears that the onions are beginning to burn. Add 1 teaspoon of olive oil if the pan becomes too dry and the bottom begins to scorch. When the onions have browned, remove them from the heat until ready to serve.

Crispy Brussels Sprouts

SERVES 4

Crispy Brussels sprouts are made of thinly sliced Brussels sprouts that are charred. A raw Brussels sprout has a strong cabbage flavor, but the char tames the bitterness and gives it a crispy bite. The addition of sweetness from the dried fruit, smokiness from the bacon, and spiciness from the chili glaze rounds out the dish. At Magnolias we fry our sprouts, but they can also be roasted or cooked in a wok.

1 1/4 pounds Brussels sprouts
Oil, for cooking
1/3 cup chopped bacon

Sweet Chili Glaze (recipe follows)
1/3 cup golden raisins
1/3 cup candied pecans

Core and quarter the Brussels sprouts.

TO FRY IN A DEEP FRYER: Heat canola or vegetable oil to 350 degrees F and cook the Brussels sprouts for 45 seconds to 1 minute until crispy. Transfer to a paper towel to drain the excess oil.

TO FRY IN A WOK: In a wok over high heat, add 3 tablespoons of peanut oil. Cook the Brussels sprouts for 5 to 7 minutes, while stirring occasionally until slightly charred and soft. Add the chopped bacon and cook for an additional minute.

TO ROAST: Preheat the oven to 350 degrees F. Lightly toss Brussels sprouts with 3 tablespoons of olive oil and roast in the oven for 20 minutes or until crispy.

After the Brussels sprouts are cooked, transfer to a bowl and toss the remaining ingredients in a bowl and serve.

Sweet Chili Glaze

MAKES 2 CUPS

1/3 cup water
1/3 cup rice wine vinegar
1/3 cup sugar
1 tablespoon sambal (use more if you like it extra spicy)
1 1/2 teaspoons minced garlic

1 teaspoon minced ginger
1 teaspoon soy sauce
1 tablespoon ketchup
2 teaspoons cornstarch, dissolved in 1 tablespoon water, mixed well

In a small saucepan, combine the water, vinegar, sugar, sambal, garlic, ginger, soy sauce, and ketchup and bring to a boil, stirring frequently. Once the sugar has dissolved, stir in the cornstarch slurry. The sauce will start to thicken. Continue cooking for 1 minute more. Remove from the heat and let the sauce cool before using. Store in a covered container in the refrigerator for up to 2 weeks.

Cheese-Encrusted Wadmalaw Sweet Onions with a Caramelized Onion and Thyme Broth

SERVES 4

If you like French onion soup, you're going to love this recipe. We feature this dish on our menu in the late spring to celebrate the sweet onions that come from nearby Wadmalaw Island farms. The roasting brings out all the sweetness in these mild but flavorful onions, which are then topped with the three-cheese combination and baked in the herb-onion broth. It's our Southern twist on a classic French dish.

Caramelized Onion and Thyme
   Broth (recipe follows)
4 whole sweet onions of choice, peeled
$1/2$ cup grated good-quality New York
   or Vermont sharp cheddar cheese
$1/4$ cup good Danish Blue or Roquefort cheese
$1/2$ cup freshly grated Parmesan cheese
1 teaspoon chopped fresh thyme

1 teaspoon chopped fresh parsley
1 teaspoon chopped fresh chives
$1/4$ teaspoon freshly ground black pepper
1 cup Chicken Broth (page 19)
2 fresh thyme sprigs or a
   sprinkle of dried thyme
1 teaspoon minced garlic
Nonstick cooking spray

Preheat the oven to 375 degrees F. Prepare the caramelized onion and thyme broth and keep warm.

Cut a cone-shaped core into the top half of each peeled onion. It should go about $1/4$ inch into the onion with a $1 1/4$-inch diameter.

In a mixing bowl, combine the cheddar, blue cheese, Parmesan, thyme, parsley, chives, and black pepper. Fill the holes in the onions with the cheese mixture, reserving some of the mixture to make a final crust. Place the onions in a 9-inch by 9-inch baking pan and add the chicken broth, thyme sprigs, and garlic. This should come up to about $1/4$-inch high on the sides of the onions.

Spray a piece of aluminum foil with nonstick cooking spray and lightly cover the pan. Do not let the foil touch the tops of the onions if possible. Place the pan on the top shelf of the oven and bake for 1 hour.

Remove the onions from the roasting broth and transfer the broth to a large bowl. Return the onions to the pan and top with the reserved cheese mixture. Broil until the cheese becomes golden brown.

Check the seasoning of the onion broth. Ladle $3/4$ cup of the onion broth into 4 shallow soup plates. Place the cheesy onions in the plates and serve.

Caramelized Onion and Thyme Broth

1 tablespoon olive oil, plus more if needed

4 cups of julienned sweet or yellow onion

2 teaspoons minced garlic

2 teaspoons chopped fresh thyme
 leaves or 1 teaspoon dried thyme

1/2 teaspoon freshly ground black pepper

2 tablespoons sherry wine
 vinegar or sherry wine

5 cups Chicken Broth (page 19)

1 tablespoon Worcestershire sauce

In a heavy-bottom stockpot over high heat, heat the olive oil until smoking. Carefully add the onions into the oil and allow the onions to cook for 1 to 2 minutes without stirring. The natural sugars in the onions will begin to caramelize and they will turn a golden color. Stir the onion and add a little more oil, 1 teaspoon at a time, if the oil has disappeared. Continue to cook, stirring frequently, until the onions are golden brown.

Reduce the heat to medium. Add the garlic, thyme, and black pepper. Cook, stirring constantly, for about 2 minutes. Add the sherry wine vinegar to deglaze the bottom of the pan and scrape up any onion caramelization. It's okay if some onions are blackened in a few places. The onions need a good caramelized color to make the broth hearty and robust.

Add the chicken broth and Worcestershire sauce. Bring the broth to a boil, reduce to a simmer, and let simmer for 10 to 15 minutes. Remove any foam that may appear and move the stockpot to the back of the stove to keep warm.

SOUPS,
SALADS,
and
DRESSINGS

Blue Crab Bisque

Like many Lowcountry favorites, everyone has their own way of making she-crab soup, and everyone's a critic: "That's not the way my mom does it," or "My dad's recipe is the best." We encourage the conversation because family traditions are what Southern cooking is all about! In our version of the classic soup, clam juice complements the crab and adds depth, while the crab roe gives it even more flavor. I hope you enjoy it!

12 tablespoons butter
1 1/2 cups celery, finely minced
1 1/2 cups onions, finely minced
1 cup all-purpose flour
4 cups clam juice, at room temperature
4 cups milk, at room temperature
1 tablespoon fresh lemon juice
2 bay leaves
1 tablespoon Worcestershire sauce
6 ounces sherry, plus more for garnishing (optional)

1/4 teaspoon mace
1/2 cup heavy cream
3/4 cup blue crab roe, picked over to remove cartilage, shell, or other matter
1 pound lump crab meat, picked over for shell and drained of any liquid
2 teaspoons fine sea salt
Pinch white pepper
4 tablespoons sliced chives, for garnishing

In a heavy-bottom saucepan over medium heat, melt the butter without browning. Add the celery and onion and cook for 1 to 2 minutes, or until the onion is translucent. Stirring constantly, sprinkle in the flour to make a roux. Reduce the heat to low and cook for 2 to 3 minutes to cook out some of the starchy flavor of the flour.

Whisk the clam juice into the warm roux and increase the heat to medium-high. Whisk vigorously as the mixture thickens. Once smooth, whisk in the milk and allow the mixture to re-thicken, continuing to whisk until smooth again. Allow this to simmer 1 to 2 minutes. Add the lemon juice, bay leaves, Worcestershire, sherry, mace, heavy cream, crab roe, and crab meat. Allow to simmer lightly for 10 to 15 minutes, stirring occasionally. Remove the bay leaves and discard. Add the salt and white pepper. Ladle the bisque into 12 bowls and garnish with chives and a few additional drops of sherry, if desired.

Creamy Tomato Bisque with Chiffonade of Fresh Basil

SERVES 8

This soup makes an elegant starter, but simple tomato soup and grilled cheese sandwiches are also hard to beat. The recipe is extra special with fresh tomatoes picked at the height of summer; however, you can use canned tomatoes depending on the season.

1/4 cup plus 1 teaspoon extra virgin olive oil
1/2 cup chopped yellow onion
1 teaspoon chopped garlic
1/2 cup flour
3 cups Chicken Broth (page 19), divided
1 chicken bouillon cube
4 cups homemade tomato sauce or
   2 (14 1/2-ounce) cans of tomato sauce
2 cups tomato juice

3 large fresh vine-ripened tomatoes, chopped, or 1 (14 1/2-ounce) can whole peeled tomatoes, crushed
3/4 cup thinly sliced fresh basil, loosely packed, divided
1 cup heavy cream
1/2 teaspoon salt
Dash white pepper
8 ounces fresh lump crab meat, picked clean of any shell (optional)

In a heavy-bottom stockpot over medium heat, heat the oil. Add the onion and garlic. Sauté for 2 to 3 minutes, stirring constantly, until the onions are translucent. Reduce the heat and make a roux by adding in the flour and stirring until well combined. Continue to cook over low heat for 5 minutes, stirring constantly. Turn the heat up to medium and add 1 1/2 cups of the chicken broth, stirring vigorously. Continue to stir until the broth begins to thicken and is smooth. Gradually add the remaining 1 1/2 cups of chicken broth and the bouillon cube, stirring constantly until the broth thickens again.

Reduce heat to low and simmer for 5 minutes to cook out the starchy flavor.

Add the tomato sauce, tomato juice, chopped tomatoes with their juices, and 1/2 cup of sliced basil. Simmer for 10 minutes. Be sure to skim off any foam that may collect on the top. Add the heavy cream, bring to a simmer, and skim again, if necessary. Add the salt and white pepper. Divide the hot soup mixture between 8 bowls. Garnish by sprinkling the crab meat (if using) and the remaining 1/4 cup of basil over the soup. Serve at once.

Elwood's Ham Chowder

This recipe has a lot of Southern ingredients—and memories—together, all in one pot. Chef Donald Barickman and his dad, Elwood, created the first version of the chowder on a cold and rainy day many years ago. It became quite popular at the restaurant and has since been featured in Martha Stewart Living, The Best American Recipes 2003–2004 *cookbook and by the Turner South network's* Blue Ribbon.

Elwood and family were from the "other Charleston," West Virginia. DB and I used to take our boys snow skiing up in the nearby Timberline area when they were growing up. Elwood's chowder was the perfect hearty supper after a day on the slopes.

1 tablespoon vegetable oil
1 pound country ham trimmings, coarsely ground or minced
3 cups medium-diced onions
2 tablespoons sliced garlic
12 cups stemmed and diced fresh collards
1 1/2 tablespoons fresh thyme
2 tablespoons chopped fresh parsley

1 (28-ounce) can whole tomatoes
7 cups Chicken Broth (page 19)
1 pint beef stock
6 cups diced red potatoes, cut in 1/4-inch dice
1 1/2 teaspoons freshly ground black pepper
1 1/2 teaspoons Tabasco, plus more to taste
Salt

In a heavy-bottom stockpot over medium heat, heat the vegetable oil. Add the ham and render the fat by cooking it slowly, stirring frequently to keep it from browning. Add the onions and garlic. Reduce the heat to low and continue to cook, stirring occasionally, until the onions and garlic are soft. You may need to add a little more oil if the onion and garlic absorb all of the rendered fat. Slowly add the collards in two batches and allow them to wilt. Add the herbs, tomatoes with their juices, chicken broth, beef stock, and potatoes. Slowly bring the mixture up to a simmer and continue to cook for 20 to 30 minutes, or until the potatoes are cooked through. Skim off any foam or oil that may appear at the top during the cooking process. Add the black pepper and Tabasco. Season to taste with salt and more Tabasco if desired.

Oyster Stew

This is a really quick Lowcountry recipe to make during the winter months. Oyster stew can be served for a casual meal, or as a starter on a special occasion. Many Charlestonians serve this as a rich and decadent Christmas Eve supper. Grab a pint of oysters from your local seafood shop and be sure to check the dates to get the freshest they have.

1 pint oysters
4 tablespoons butter
1 large leek (white portion only), diced
2 garlic cloves, minced
1/4 teaspoon red pepper flakes
1/4 teaspoon paprika

1/4 teaspoon kosher salt
1/2 teaspoon freshly ground black pepper
6 cups half-and-half
1 teaspoon chopped fresh
   parsley, for garnishing
Saltines or oyster crackers, for serving

Drain the oysters and reserve the liquor (liquid). Be sure to check the oysters for shells.

In a heavy-bottom saucepan over medium heat, melt the butter. Add the leek and sauté until wilted, about 3 minutes. Add the garlic and continue to cook for another 2 minutes. Be sure not to let the garlic brown. Add the red pepper flakes, paprika, salt, and black pepper; stir well. The spices should get lightly toasted. Reduce the heat to low and add the half-and-half, oysters, and reserved oyster liquor.

Cook over low heat until warm throughout; don't bring it to a boil. Garnish with the parsley and season with additional salt and pepper if desired. Serve with Saltines or oyster crackers.

Black Bean Chili with Scallion and Cilantro Sour Cream

SERVES 16

This delicious chili is off the very first Magnolias menu, and it rose to fame, winning the 1991 South Carolina Chili Cook-Off contest. The recipe differs from traditional chili and features roasted pork and black beans. Ginger and jalapeño give it a nice kick that is balanced by the scallion and cilantro sour cream. I think this is a great dish to make for a fall football weekend.

1/4 cup olive oil

4 cups roughly chopped yellow onions

4 tablespoons minced garlic

5 tablespoons peeled and minced fresh ginger, divided

2 tablespoons minced jalapeño

Roasted Pork (page 74)

5 cups Chicken Broth (page 19)

2 smoked pork neck bones

6 ounces tomato paste

Black Beans (page 74)

2 teaspoons freshly ground black pepper, divided

1 tablespoon cumin

2 tablespoons chopped cilantro

Scallion and Cilantro Sour Cream (page 74)

In a heavy-bottom pot over medium heat, heat the oil. Add the onion, garlic, 4 tablespoons of ginger, and the minced jalapeño and sauté while stirring for 2 to 3 minutes, until the onions are translucent. Add the pork, chicken broth, neck bones, tomato paste, the reserved juices from the browned pork, and the juices from the black beans. Let the pork and vegetables simmer over low heat for 40 minutes, or until the pork is quite tender, but not stringy. Add the cooked black beans, 1 teaspoon of black pepper, and the cumin. Cook uncovered for 10 to 15 minutes over low heat until the flavors meld and the consistency of chili is reached. Remove the neck bones and discard.

Five minutes prior to serving the chili, add the cilantro, the remaining 1 tablespoon of ginger, and the remaining 1 teaspoon of black pepper and continue to cook over low heat in order to preserve the fresh flavors until ready to serve.

Pour the chili into warm soup bowls and add a dollop of the scallion and cilantro sour cream on top of each bowl.

continued »

Roasted Pork

MAKES 3 ½ POUNDS

1 (5-pound) pork shoulder or Boston
  butt, trimmed of all fat and sinew
  or well-trimmed and coarsely
  ground by the butcher

1 tablespoon olive oil
1 tablespoon minced garlic
2 tablespoons freshly ground black pepper

Preheat the oven to 450 degrees F.

Cut the pork shoulder in ½-inch dice or smaller. Lightly toss the pork with the olive oil, garlic, and black pepper. Evenly spread the pork out onto 2 baking sheets with raised edges to hold the juices. Roast the pork for approximately 1 hour, or until the meat is nicely browned, but not black. Remove the pork, reserving all of the juices and brown bits on the baking sheets. When the pork is cool, break it into the diced pieces again and reserve.

Black Beans

MAKES 2 QUARTS

4 cups dried black beans or 4 (15-ounce)
  cans, drained but not rinsed

16 cups Chicken Broth (page 19)

Pour the dried black beans onto a baking sheet. Pick through them to look for small pebbles and discolored beans and then transfer to a colander and rinse.

In a heavy-bottom saucepan over high heat, bring the beans and chicken broth to a boil. Reduce to a simmer and cook for about 2 hours, or until the beans are very soft but before their skins start to break. Add water if needed, 1 cup at a time. Strain the beans over a large pot or bowl to catch the juices and reserve.

Scallion and Cilantro Sour Cream

MAKES 1 ¼ CUPS

1 cup sour cream
2 tablespoons minced scallions
1 tablespoon minced red bell pepper
½ teaspoon minced garlic

1 tablespoon chopped fresh cilantro
½ teaspoon cumin
½ teaspoon salt
¼ teaspoon freshly ground black pepper

In a large bowl, combine all the ingredients and mix well. Serve at once or transfer to a covered storage container and refrigerate for up to 1 week.

Johns Island Asparagus Salad with Deviled Eggs, Pancetta, Arugula, Pine Nuts, and Green Goddess Dressing

SERVES 6

Across the river from Charleston, Johns Island boasts some of the Lowcountry's most fertile farmland. Asparagus is a wonderful local springtime crop that we often serve at the restaurant. The green goddess dressing is our best effort at replicating the original 1920s classic from San Francisco's famous Palace Hotel. I decided not to add garlic to my recipe—because, according to legend, you're supposed to rub the garlic along the inside of the salad bowl and tear the lettuce by hand.

1/3 pound pancetta, diced
2 tablespoons butter
2 bunches asparagus spears, cut
   diagonally into 3/4–inch pieces
3/4 cup thinly sliced leeks,
   white and green parts

12 Deviled Eggs (recipe follows)
1 1/2 pounds arugula, washed and spun dry
1 cup Green Goddess Dressing (page 76)
1/3 cup pine nuts, for garnishing
Coarse sea salt
Freshly ground black pepper

In a large skillet over medium-high heat, sauté the pancetta until crispy. Remove from the pan and keep warm. Add the butter to the same pan, along with the asparagus and leeks, keeping them separate. Sauté the asparagus and leeks until tender, 2 to 3 minutes. Remove from heat and keep warm.

On the base of each of 6 large salad plates, evenly divide the leeks. Crisscross the asparagus spears like a herringbone necklace in the center of the plate. Place 1 deviled egg on each side of the plate.

In a large bowl, combine the arugula and dressing and toss lightly. Equally divide the arugula among the plates, placing a handful on top of the asparagus. Garnish with the pancetta and pine nuts. Season with salt and pepper to taste.

Deviled Eggs

MAKES 12 DEVILED EGGS

6 eggs
3 tablespoons Duke's mayonnaise
2 tablespoons sweet pickle relish

1 teaspoon prepared mustard
Pinch salt

continued »

Place the eggs in a medium saucepan, cover with cold water, and bring to a boil. Cover the pan, remove it from the heat, and let sit for 12 minutes. Drain the water, then shake the eggs back and forth in the drained pan to start cracking the shells. Peel under cold running water and set aside.

Halve the eggs and carefully remove the yolks. Put the yolks in a small bowl and mash with a fork, stirring in the mayonnaise, relish, mustard, and salt. Using a spoon or piping bag, fill the egg whites with the mixture. Transfer the eggs to a large plate and refrigerate until ready to serve.

Green Goddess Dressing

MAKES 3 CUPS

2 teaspoons anchovy paste, or 3 to 4 oil-packed anchovies, rinsed and chopped
1/2 Hass avocado, peeled
3/4 cup Duke's mayonnaise
1/3 cup sour cream or crème fraîche
1/3 cup buttermilk
1/2 cup chopped fresh flat-leaf parsley
1/4 cup chopped fresh tarragon
3 tablespoons chopped fresh chives
2 tablespoons freshly squeezed lemon juice
1 tablespoon tarragon vinegar
1/2 teaspoon coarse sea salt
1/2 teaspoon freshly ground black pepper

In a food processor or blender, combine all of the ingredients and process for about 10 seconds, until the mixture is smooth and green. Taste and adjust seasoning as needed.

Thin with a little water if needed. Store in a covered container in the refrigerator for up to 1 week.

Summer Tomato and Vidalia Onion Salad

SERVES 4

This quick salad is summertime at its best. Beautiful vine-ripened tomatoes topped with marinated Vidalia onions—it's a wonderful way to enjoy the season's bountiful produce. Seek out your local farmers' market or roadside stands for the very best tomatoes.

2 peak-of-the-season tomatoes
Vidalia Onion Salad (recipe follows)
1 tablespoon fresh Italian parsley
    chiffonade, for garnishing
1 teaspoon coarse sea salt, for garnishing

Gently rinse the tomatoes with cold water and hand dry. Slice the tomatoes into $1/8$ inch-thin rounds and arrange on a serving platter in a circle of overlapping slices. Place a little nest of the Vidalia onion salad in the center of the tomatoes. Drizzle some of the salad marinade on top and sprinkle with the parsley and sea salt.

Vidalia Onion Salad

MAKES 2 CUPS

2 cups thinly sliced Vidalia onion rings
2 tablespoons Duke's mayonnaise
3 tablespoons white vinegar
1 tablespoon sugar

$1/8$ teaspoon fine sea salt
2 tablespoons extra-virgin olive oil
Dash white pepper

In a large bowl, toss together all of the ingredients. Put the salad in the refrigerator and allow to marinate for 20 minutes to 1 hour.

Salmon BLT Salad

This is an over-the-top salad, and I can imagine serving it for lunch on a screened porch in the warmer seasons. The vinaigrette has a summer flair with the addition of Vidalia onion. I also like to substitute or add things like tomatoes, avocados, and a variety of seasonal fresh herbs or fruits.

6 (4- to 5-ounce) salmon fillets
3 tablespoons olive oil, divided
Coarse sea salt
Freshly cracked black pepper
6 (1/2-inch-thick) slices ciabatta
    bread or French baguette
12 pieces applewood-smoked bacon
2 teaspoons Roasted Garlic
    Purée (page 82)

1 (3/4 pound) log goat cheese,
    sliced into 6 rounds
3/4 pound arugula
3/4 cup Lemon Caper Vinaigrette
    (page 82), divided
3 large beefsteak tomatoes,
    each cut into 4 slices
1/2 small red onion, julienned

In a medium bowl, lightly coat the salmon fillets with 1 tablespoon of olive oil and season with salt and pepper.

Brush the bread with the remaining 2 tablespoons of olive oil and sprinkle with salt and pepper.

Use a large skillet over medium heat and cook the bacon until crispy. Remove the bacon from the pan; pour off the drippings and save for later use. Place the brushed bread into the pan and toast both sides. Top each slice with roasted garlic purée and a slice of goat cheese and remove from the pan. Keep warm.

In the same pan, sear the salmon on both sides for about 3 minutes. Remove from the heat and keep warm. (If using a grill, preheat to 350 degrees F and place the fillets at an angle toward 2 o'clock; in 2 minutes rotate them to 9 o'clock. Turn the fillets over and repeat the same rotating process. This process helps create nice grill marks on the fish).

In a medium bowl, lightly toss the arugula with 1/3 cup vinaigrette.

Place 1 piece of bread in the middle of each of the 6 plates, then crisscross 2 slices of bacon on top. On top of that, place a small handful of arugula, a tomato slice, more arugula, another tomato, then more arugula. Top with the fish. We use a decorative sweetgrass toothpick to hold it in place. Finish each stack with a pinch of red onions on top. Use a small spoon to drizzle the remaining vinaigrette around the edge of the plate for garnish.

continued »

Roasted Garlic Purée

MAKES ½ TO ⅔ CUP

The easiest way to make roasted garlic is on a baking sheet with raised sides, using cloves that have already been peeled. Peeled garlic cloves are readily available in the produce section of most grocery stores; they're sold in bags, cartons, or plastic containers. This purée freezes well.

2 cups whole peeled garlic cloves
¼ cup olive oil

Salt
Freshly ground black pepper

Preheat the oven to 375 degrees F.

In a baking pan, ovenproof dish, or baking sheet with raised sides, spread out the garlic cloves and drizzle with olive oil. Add enough water to the pan to cover the garlic. Bake in the oven for 25 minutes, or until the water has evaporated and the garlic cloves are golden brown and soft. Transfer the garlic to a food processor and purée. Season with salt and pepper to taste. Store in an airtight container and refrigerate for up to 2 weeks.

Lemon Caper Vinaigrette

MAKES 4 CUPS

¼ cup finely diced Vidalia onion
1 cup freshly squeezed lemon juice
¼ cup honey
2 tablespoons Dijon mustard
1 cup extra virgin olive oil
1 cup canola oil
¼ cup capers

1 cup peeled, seeded, and diced tomatoes
¼ cup finely diced red bell
   pepper (about ½ pepper)
¼ cup minced fresh chives
1 tablespoon sea salt
1 tablespoon freshly ground black pepper

In a bowl, combine the onion and lemon juice and let sit for about 10 minutes.

Add the honey and Dijon mustard. Slowly pour in the olive oil and canola oil, steadily whisking to combine. Add the capers, tomatoes, bell pepper, and chives. Transfer to a Mason jar with a tight-fitting lid and give it a couple good shakes before using. Refrigerate for up to 1 week.

Note: If you don't plan on using the vinaigrette right away, add the minced chives right before serving to retain their color.

Iceberg Wedge Salad with Buttermilk, Basil, and Blue Cheese Dressing, Country Ham Cracklings, and Grape Tomatoes SERVES 6

You will find this simple, classic salad on a lot of Southern menus these days. Our recipe is a little different. We use country ham instead of bacon, and buttermilk adds a tangy twist to a traditional blue cheese dressing.

1 large head iceberg lettuce, picked of
    its outer leaves, cut into 6 wedges
Buttermilk, Basil, and Blue Cheese
    Dressing (page 89)

Country Ham Cracklings (page 52)
$1/2$ pint grape tomatoes, for garnishing

Place the wedges of iceberg lettuce on each of 6 chilled plates and spoon a few tablespoons of the dressing over them. Sprinkle the wedges with the ham cracklings, garnish with the grape tomatoes, and serve immediately.

Shrimp and Crab Salad

SERVES 4

Shrimp and Crab Salad is nice to make to keep around for lunch or dinner in a hurry. This recipe is universal; you can also substitute lobster, scallops, or imitation crab—all will work fine. Use lettuce cups, hollowed out tomatoes, avocado or a mix of lettuces for the salad, or serve it with crackers or on a croissant.

1/2 lemon
1/2 pound raw shrimp, 51/60 count,
    peeled and deveined
1/2 pound fresh jumbo lump or
    imitation crab meat
1/2 cup finely diced celery
3 tablespoons finely diced red onion

1/2 teaspoon Old Bay Seasoning
2 teaspoons fresh lemon juice
1/2 cup Duke's mayonnaise
1 1/2 tablespoons chopped fresh dill
Salt
Freshly ground black pepper

Bring a 2-quart stock pot of water to a boil and add the lemon. Add the shrimp to the pot and cook for about 2 minutes or until pink. Strain the shrimp and transfer to a bowl of ice water to stop the cooking. After 10 minutes, drain the shrimp again and pat dry.

In a small bowl, combine the shrimp, crab, celery, onion, Old Bay, lemon juice, and mayonnaise and toss gently. Add the dill and season with salt and pepper to taste. Cover and refrigerate until ready to use.

Grilled Chicken Salad with Caramelized Onions, Lemon–Herb Vinaigrette, and Fresh Parmesan over Mixed Greens

MAKES 4 SERVINGS

This simple-yet-elegant salad is great for a group luncheon or a supper for two. It's been on Magnolias' menu for many years. Back in the kitchen, you always knew our founder, Tom Parsell Sr., was having lunch when you saw a ticket come in adding bacon to the salad. It was one of his favorites.

1 teaspoon soy sauce
1 teaspoon olive oil
¼ teaspoon dried oregano
¼ teaspoon dried thyme
¼ teaspoon dried basil
¼ teaspoon onion powder
¼ teaspoon garlic powder
¼ teaspoon freshly ground black
   pepper, plus more for serving

1 pound boneless skinless chicken
   breast, 4 ounces each
1 pound mixed lettuces
Lemon–Herb Vinaigrette (recipe follows)
2 cups Caramelized Onions (page 61)
Edible flower blossoms (optional)
Freshly shaved Parmesan cheese

In a bowl large enough to hold the chicken, combine the soy sauce, olive oil, oregano, thyme, basil, onion powder, garlic powder, and black pepper. Toss the chicken with the marinade and refrigerate for 4 hours or overnight. If necessary, this can be done right before grilling.

Fire the grill.

Place the chicken breasts on the hot grill, close the lid, and grill them for 3 to 4 minutes on each side. Remove the chicken and allow the pieces to rest for a minute before you slice them.

To serve the salads, toss the lettuces lightly with the vinaigrette. Mound about 2 cups of lettuces per full-size plate. Top each with the slices of chicken and the caramelized onions. Sprinkle with the petals of edible flower blossoms (if desired), grated fresh Parmesan, and a grind of black pepper.

Lemon–Herb Vinaigrette

MAKES 1½ CUPS

2 tablespoons Dijon mustard
2 tablespoons apple cider vinegar
¼ cup fresh lemon juice
1 cup olive oil
2 tablespoons chopped fresh parsley

2 tablespoons chopped fresh chives
2 tablespoons finely julienned then
   lightly chopped fresh basil
1 teaspoon minced garlic
¼ teaspoon freshly ground black pepper

continued »

The emulsion for this dressing can be easily done by mixing the mustard, vinegar, and lemon juice in a blender. Next, turn the blender on low speed and slowly stream in the oil, running the blender for only 30 to 40 seconds. The blender method will give you a creamier, fluffier dressing. After blending, pour the vinaigrette into a bowl. With a whisk, fold in the herbs, garlic, and black pepper.

If making the dressing by hand, whisk together the mustard, vinegar, and lemon juice in a glass or stainless-steel bowl. Add the oil very slowly in a steady stream, whisking vigorously until all the oil is incorporated. Fold in the herbs, garlic, and black pepper.

Use immediately or store the dressing, covered, in a glass or stainless-steel container in the refrigerator. It should keep for a day or two before the ingredients separate. If this does occur, the dressing can simply be remixed before dressing the salads.

Lemon Lingonberry Vinaigrette

Commonly called a "mountain cranberry," lingonberry has a slightly sweet and acidic taste. This dressing was served for many years with Magnolias' house salad. We also use it with poultry and pork dishes. You can find lingonberry conserve at your better grocery stores. Here at the restaurant, we use our lemon-herb vinaigrette as a "mother" base for several of our salad dressings—including this one—simply adding different herbs or fruit to change the flavor profile.

Lemon–Herb Vinaigrette (page 87)
1/3 cup lingonberry conserve

When making the lemon-herb vinaigrette, add the lingonberry conserve to the vinaigrette along with the herbs.

Buttermilk, Basil, and Blue Cheese Dressing

MAKES 1 3/4 CUPS

This is a longtime favorite recipe which we regularly use for our wedge salads. I'm partial to Duke's mayonnaise and a fan of Clemson blue cheese—both are big on flavor and produced in the upstate of South Carolina. Of course, feel free to use your own preferred products. This dressing also makes a good dip for vegetables.

1/4 cup Duke's mayonnaise
1/4 cup sour cream
3/4 cup buttermilk
1/4 teaspoon minced garlic
1/4 teaspoon salt
2 tablespoons honey
2 tablespoons apple cider vinegar

1 tablespoon plus 2 teaspoons
   julienned fresh basil
1 cup Roquefort, Danish blue cheese,
   or Clemson blue cheese, crumbled
   but not mashed, divided
Freshly ground black pepper

In a bowl, lightly whisk the mayonnaise, sour cream, buttermilk, garlic, salt, honey, and vinegar until smooth. Gently fold in the basil and 1/2 cup of blue cheese. Season to taste with pepper and more salt, if desired.

Note: After the lettuce is tossed in the dressing and put on salad plates, sprinkle the top of the salads with the remaining 1/2 cup of blue cheese.

Ned's Yellow Cab Dressing

Ned was a legendary chef who used to have a restaurant called Cab Company down in St. Augustine, Florida. He cooked in the school of Alice Waters—fresh and local. This dressing is delicious on any salad and with vegetables, beans, and grains. Try adding a little to your hummus. The recipe gets its unique flavor from brewer's yeast, which is available in most grocery stores in the baking or spice sections.

$1/3$ cup tamari
$1/4$ cup apple cider vinegar
2 tablespoons fresh lemon juice
2 tablespoons tahini or sesame seed paste
2 large garlic cloves

$1 1/4$ cup brewer's yeast or nutritional yeast
2 teaspoons sesame oil
$1 3/4$ cup safflower oil
1 cup water

In a food processor or blender, process the tamari, vinegar, lemon juice, tahini, garlic, brewer's yeast, and sesame oil until smooth. Slowly stream in the safflower oil, then add water as needed. Transfer to an airtight container and refrigerate until ready to use. This dressing will keep for up to 2 weeks in the refrigerator.

BRUNCH
and
SANDWICHES

Chicken and Sage Hash with Poached Eggs and a Cracked Peppercorn Hollandaise

SERVES 4

This recipe has been a breakfast staple in my house for years. It's easy to put together and works great for a crowd. The hash can even be done the night before, so that you just poach the eggs in the morning. I prefer homemade hollandaise, but if you're tight on time, you can always buy the package to make this sauce. It's in the spice section of every grocery store.

4 tablespoons plus 1 teaspoon
   olive oil, divided

3 cups skin-on diced baking potatoes, cut
   into 1/4-inch dice (about 3 potatoes)

1/4 teaspoon salt, plus more to taste

1/2 teaspoon freshly ground black
   pepper, plus more to taste

1/2 cup roughly diced yellow onion

1/2 cup roughly diced celery, no leaves

1/2 cup roughly diced red pepper

1 teaspoon minced garlic

6 boneless, skinless chicken thighs

3 cups chopped spinach

1 tablespoon chopped fresh sage
   or 1 1/2 teaspoons dried sage

8 Poached Eggs (page 94)

Cracked Peppercorn Hollandaise
   (page 94)

Preheat the oven to 425 degrees F.

In a bowl, combine 1 tablespoon of the olive oil, the potatoes, salt, and black pepper and mix well. Transfer to a heavy baking sheet with sides and place on the top shelf of the oven. Bake for 15 to 20 minutes, stirring once, until the potatoes are a light golden color. Set aside.

In a heavy-bottom skillet over medium high heat, heat 2 tablespoons of olive oil. Add the onion, celery, red pepper, and garlic and sauté while stirring, 2 to 3 minutes, or until the onions are translucent. Remove from the heat and let cool.

Rub the chicken with 1 teaspoon of olive oil and a sprinkle of salt and black pepper.

Transfer the thighs to a baking sheet and roast for 25 to 30 minutes, or until the internal temperature reaches 175 degrees F. Cool to room temperature and rough chop the meat.

When ready to serve, heat the remaining 1 tablespoon of olive oil in a nonstick frying pan over medium heat. Add the potatoes, vegetables, chopped chicken, and spinach and toss for 3 to 5 minutes. Add the sage along with salt and pepper to taste.

Evenly divide the hash among 4 soup bowls. Place 2 poached eggs on top of each bowl of hash and spoon the cracked peppercorn hollandaise on top.

continued »

Poached Eggs

12 cups water
8 eggs

4 tablespoons white or apple cider vinegar

In a deep, heavy-bottom pan, heat the water to a simmer just below the boiling point. Give the water a swirl with a spatula. Crack the eggs one by one into a cup, then gently slide them into the water. The eggs will poach with the water temperature at just below a simmer but with bubbles still breaking to the top occasionally.

The cooking times should be:
    3 minutes for runny yolk
    4 minutes for medium yolk
    5 minutes for hard yolk

Remove the eggs from the water with a slotted spoon and serve.

Cracked Peppercorn Hollandaise

4 egg yolks
1 tablespoon fresh lemon juice
1/4 teaspoon salt
3 dashes Tabasco
3 tablespoons water

1 pound unsalted butter, melted
1 tablespoon chopped fresh parsley
1 teaspoon freshly cracked black pepper
Cayenne pepper (optional)

In a stainless-steel bowl or in the bowl of an electric mixer, mix the egg yolks, lemon juice, salt, Tabasco, and water. Place the bowl over a simmering pot of water, double-boiler style, taking care not to touch the water. Whisk the yolk mixture vigorously for 3 to 4 minutes until it triples in volume and becomes opaque and pale yellow in color. It may be necessary to take the bowl off of the stove a couple of times to release the steam that builds up.

Remove the bowl from over the simmering water and place it on the counter on a damp cloth to steady it or on the mixer with the whip attachment. Whisking vigorously, pour in the melted butter in a slow, steady stream. The melted butter should be the same temperature as the warm yolk mixture for a tight emulsification. After all of the butter is added, fold in the parsley and cracked black pepper.

Taste the sauce and adjust the seasoning with salt, lemon juice, Tabasco, or cayenne pepper (if using). Serve at once, or transfer the hollandaise to a small glass bowl and keep it in a warm place for about an hour before serving. To successfully hold together, the hollandaise should remain at a warm temperature, becoming neither too hot nor too cold.

Note: When melting the butter for the hollandaise, do it very slowly. Otherwise, the butter will boil and the water in it will cause the golden liquid butter to emulsify with the water, which inhibits the butter's ability to thicken. Let the melted butter settle and pour or ladle the golden butter from the top, leaving the water and the milk solids to be discarded. The result is what is known as "clarified butter."

Banana Pudding–Stuffed French Toast with Peanut Butter Syrup

SERVES 6

This French toast is over-the-top crispy, gooey, and delicious, all in one. A riff on the beloved peanut butter and banana sandwich, it's one of Magnolias' most popular brunch dishes. When we try to swap it off the menu, our regulars always ask for it to come back!

6 (1½-inch-thick) slices brioche bread
Banana Pudding (recipe follows)
Egg Wash (recipe follows)
French Toast Crust (page 98)

Peanut Butter Syrup (page 98)
12 slices applewood–smoked
  bacon, for serving
Sliced banana, for serving

Cut a 1-inch slit into one side of each slice of brioche. Using a piping bag with a star tip, pipe 2 tablespoons of banana pudding into the brioche. Next, soak each slice of brioche in the egg wash and then dredge it in the French toast crust mixture.

Preheat the oven to 350 degrees F. Grease a baking sheet with butter, arrange the brioche, and cook for 6 minutes on each side, until golden brown.

To finish, top with the peanut butter syrup and serve with two slices of applewood-smoked bacon and sliced banana.

Banana Pudding

MAKES 1½ CUPS

1 (8-ounce) package cream cheese, softened
¼ cup sugar
3 bananas, mashed

In a bowl, mix together the cream cheese and sugar until smooth, then add the mashed bananas. Mix until well incorporated.

Egg Wash

MAKES 2 CUPS

6 large eggs
1 cup heavy (whipping) cream
2 teaspoons kosher salt
½ teaspoon ground cinnamon
1 teaspoon vanilla extract

In a medium bowl, whip the eggs, cream, salt, cinnamon, and vanilla extract together to combine.

continued »

French Toast Crust

4 cups crushed vanilla wafers
4 cups crushed cornflakes

In a food processor, purée the vanilla wafers and cornflakes until smooth.

Peanut Butter Syrup

1 cup smooth peanut butter
1 cup Karo light corn syrup

In a small bowl, whisk together the peanut butter and corn syrup until smooth.

Chicken-Fried Steak with Caramelized Onion and White Cheddar Grits, Fried Eggs, Buttermilk Biscuits, and Cracked Pepper Gravy

SERVES 6

A Southern staple, chicken-fried steak is typically deep-fried in a cast-iron skillet and served with a cream gravy. The recipe gets its name from the preparation for frying—the milk-and-egg batter is similar to what you'd use to fry chicken. I prefer to use cube steak in this recipe for the mouthfeel it adds. When this dish comes together with a salty, peppery finish from the gravy, it's really special!

continued »

3 tablespoons all-purpose flour
1 teaspoon smoked paprika
1 teaspoon baking soda
2 teaspoons baking powder
1 1/2 teaspoons freshly ground black pepper
1 tablespoon sea salt
1 teaspoon granulated garlic
3 cups buttermilk
2 tablespoons Texas Pete hot sauce

13 eggs, divided
6 slices cube steak
Vegetable or canola oil, for frying
   (enough to fill your skillet halfway)
Butter, for frying the eggs
Caramelized Onion and White
   Cheddar Grits (page 58)
Cracked Pepper Gravy (recipe follows)
Buttermilk Biscuits (page 29)

In a shallow pan or bowl, combine the flour, paprika, baking soda, baking powder, pepper, salt, and garlic and mix well. Reserve 4 tablespoons of the flour mixture for the cracked pepper gravy. In another bowl, mix together the buttermilk, hot sauce, and one egg. Put the cube steaks in the flour mixture and coat well, shaking off any excess flour. Next, dip the steaks into the buttermilk mixture, then dredge in the flour a second time to coat the steaks thoroughly.

Heat the oil in a large, deep skillet over medium-high heat and carefully fry 2 or 3 steaks at a time, depending on the size of the skillet. Cook until golden brown, about 3 minutes per side. Remove from the pan and keep warm. Reserve 4 tablespoons of oil for the cracked pepper gravy.

Prepare the grits, gravy, and biscuits.

In a separate large skillet over medium heat, melt the butter. Fry the remaining 12 eggs to the desired doneness. (At the restaurant, we serve the eggs over easy.)

To finish the dish, spoon 1/2 cup of grits onto the left side of each plate. Top with the steak and drizzle with gravy. Place 2 eggs on the right side of each plate and finish with the biscuit.

Cracked Pepper Gravy

MAKES 1 1/2 CUPS

4 tablespoons of oil, reserved
   from Chicken-Fried Steak
4 tablespoons dredging flour mixture,
   reserved from Chicken-Fried Steak

1 cup milk
1/2 cup heavy (whipping) cream
1 tablespoon freshly cracked black pepper
Salt

In a sauté pan over medium heat, heat the reserved oil. Whisk in the flour mixture and cook until the color turns light brown. Whisk in the milk until smooth, about 5 minutes. Reduce the heat to low and add the cream while continuing to whisk until desired consistency. Season with cracked pepper and salt to taste. Remove from heat and keep warm until ready to serve.

Cinnamon Rolls

It's hard passing a big baking sheet of cinnamon rolls when they are coming out of the oven! We serve these for Sunday brunch, and they're always a hit. Consider making this recipe at home for a house party or special holiday breakfast.

2 cups milk
3 tablespoons dry yeast
2/3 cup granulated sugar
3 sticks butter melted, divided
3 eggs, divided
4 to 8 cups all–purpose flour, divided

2 teaspoons salt
1 teaspoon water
Cinnamon Sugar (recipe follows)
Nonstick cooking spray
Vanilla Glaze (recipe follows)

Gently warm the milk to 100 degrees F.

Combine the yeast, sugar, 1 stick of melted butter, the warmed milk, and 2 eggs in the bowl of a 6-quart mixer fitted with a whisk attachment. Let sit until yeast is activated and it bubbles up on the surface.

Add 4 cups of all-purpose flour and the salt and mix with a dough hook attachment until incorporated. Begin adding the remaining flour a little at a time until dough is slightly sticky. You may not need to use all of the remaining flour. The dough should still be slightly sticky, but not overly so. Cover the bowl with plastic wrap and allow the dough to proof until doubled in size, 30 minutes to 1 hour.

Preheat the oven to 350 degrees F. Roll out dough into a large square, about 1/8 inch thick.

Whisk the remaining 1 egg with the water and brush the top inch of the square with the egg wash. Brush the rest of the dough with the remaining 2 sticks of melted butter, then cover generously with cinnamon sugar, making sure not to sprinkle any on the egg wash.

Begin rolling up the dough, starting at the edge of the dough closest to you. Make sure to gently tuck the dough in as you roll to ensure a nice, tight roll. Slice into 12 rolls. Place the cinnamon rolls about an inch apart on a baking sheet lined with parchment paper then sprayed with nonstick cooking spray, with one in the middle. Cover with plastic wrap. Proof the buns until they have doubled in size and are touching. Bake for 10 minutes, or until lightly golden brown. Drizzle with vanilla glaze and serve.

Cinnamon Sugar

4 cups granulated sugar
1/4 cup ground cinnamon

In a large bowl, mix the cinnamon and sugar together until well combined.

Vanilla Glaze

MAKES 4 CUPS

3 cups powdered sugar, sifted
1 1/4 cups heavy (whipping) cream
2 teaspoons vanilla extract

Sift the powdered sugar into a large bowl, then whisk in the heavy cream and vanilla extract until combined.

Fried Green Tomato BLT

MAKES 4 SANDWICHES

The fried green tomato BLT is truly a great sandwich! A Magnolias signature dish, we sell four to five dozen of these a day, and it keeps the pantry chef hustling. Be sure to use good-quality bacon if it's available. My favorite is Nueske's. It's from Wisconsin, but it works great in Southern recipes. Otherwise, most applewood- or pecan-smoked bacon will work.

The trick to getting a glaze on a toasted sandwich is to apply a really thin layer of mayonnaise on the toast. After you've flipped the slice of bread on the griddle, turn it over again on each side to crisp up the mayo.

2 tablespoons melted butter or mayonnaise
8 slices jalapeño cornbread or
   8 slices Texas toast
2 cups Pimiento Cheese (page 49)

12 slices Fried Green Tomatoes (page 57)
16 Nueske's applewood–smoked
   bacon slices, cooked
1 head red leaf lettuce, chilled

Butter and griddle both sides of the bread. Spread a thin layer of pimiento cheese on one side of each piece of bread. Lay the cheese sides up and top half of the slices with 3 slices of fried green tomatoes, 4 of slices bacon, and 3 leaves of red leaf lettuce. Place the remaining slices of bread on top, cheese-side down. Carefully cut the sandwich in half using a serrated knife. Place a toothpick in each half to hold it together. Enjoy!

Roasted Prime Rib Sandwich with Caramelized Onions, Roasted Garlic Mayo, and Provolone Piccante Cheese Served on a French Baguette

SERVES 6

This is one of my favorite hearty hot sandwiches to make. Be sure to use a nice crusty French bread.

2 French baguettes
1 cup Roasted Garlic Mayo (recipe follows)
3 pounds thinly sliced roasted
   Prime Rib (page 169)
2 cups Caramelized Onions (page 61)

12 slices provolone piccante cheese
1 pound mixed greens
12 slices tomato
Salt
Freshly ground black pepper

Preheat the oven to 425 degrees F. Cut the baguettes into thirds and then slice lengthwise for a top and bottom half. Spread mayo liberally on both sides. Place 8 ounces of prime rib on the bottom half of each baguette. Top with the caramelized onions, then the provolone cheese, slightly overlapping each piece of cheese. Place the top and bottom pieces of the baguettes in the oven and bake until the bread is toasted and the cheese has melted. Remove from the oven and top with the mixed greens and tomatoes. Finish with salt and pepper to taste. Add the top half to each baguette and serve.

Roasted Garlic Mayo

MAKES 1¼ CUPS

1 cup mayonnaise of choice
2 tablespoons Roasted Garlic
   Purée (page 82)
1 teaspoon lemon juice

Kosher salt
Freshly cracked black pepper
½ teaspoon smoked paprika
2 teaspoons whole-grain mustard

In a small mixing bowl, mix together all the ingredients. Store in an airtight container and refrigerate until ready to use.

Barbecue Pork Sliders with Classic Potato Fries

Home-cooked barbecue has come a long way over the years. What started out as pork butt or pork shoulder thrown on the grill in the backyard for several hours has turned into a science. Cooking methods are divided among different regions of the country, as well as the wood you use, the cut of meat, the rub, and, of course, the sauce.

I really enjoy getting the opportunity to meet some of the country's best pit masters when they come for the Charleston Wine + Food event held each March. It's wonderful to taste their different barbecue styles and participate in the debate!

My favorite way to cook pork shoulder is on the grill over indirect heat, low and slow. Included in this recipe is an oven method that also produces great results. We serve the sliders on soft square potato rolls or Hawaiian rolls.

1 (6– to 7–pound) pork shoulder
3 to 4 tablespoons Sweet-and-Hot Pork
   Shoulder and Rib Rub (page 24)

Barbecue Sauce (page 110)
12 fresh slider–size potato rolls
Classic Potato Fries (page 110)

To cook on a grill or smoker, see the instructions for Hickory-Smoked Pork Shoulder (page 151).

To cook in the oven, preheat the oven to 350 degrees F.

Rub the pork with the rub. Place the pork in the oven and roast for 1 hour. Reduce the temperature to 210 degrees F and continue to roast for about 10 hours or until an internal temperature of 190 degrees F is reached. At this point, the meat is done and tender enough to pull apart.

Reserve the juices to put in the barbecue sauce: Remove as much of the grease as possible from the roasting pan, then deglaze the pan with a little water. Pour this into a container and put it into the refrigerator. When the grease comes to the top and solidifies, discard it and use the pure juice to give more depth and flavor to the sauce.

After the pork is cool enough to handle, pull the meat apart, discarding the shoulder bone, if present, and any pockets of heavy fat. Lightly chop the meat and put in a skillet over low heat; add some of the barbecue sauce to moisten the tender meat. Divide the soft dinner rolls into top and bottom halves and warm in the oven to lightly toast the edges. Scoop the barbecue onto the bottom half of the roll, and top with the other half. Serve with fries.

continued »

Barbecue Sauce

This is a cross between a traditional barbecue sauce and a mopping sauce. Add the pan drippings from the roasted pork if you cook it in the oven. If you desire a less tangy sauce, only use 3/4 cup of the vinegar and add 3/4 cup Chicken Broth (page 19). It works well with any pork, ribs, or chicken. This sauce can be heated and tossed with freshly pulled pork barbecue, or served in a bowl on the side.

1 1/2 cups apple cider vinegar
1/4 cup Dijon mustard
1 cup ketchup
2 tablespoons Worcestershire sauce
1 teaspoon freshly ground black pepper

1 tablespoon Tabasco
1/4 cup blackstrap molasses
2 tablespoons dark brown sugar
1/2 cup pan drippings (optional)

In a heavy-bottom saucepan over medium heat, combine all the ingredients. Simmer them for 5 minutes to meld the flavors. The sauce should be just thick enough to coat a spoon. Use immediately or allow to cool at room temperature, then cover and refrigerate. The sauce will keep for about 1 week in the refrigerator if it has pan drippings in it, or for several weeks if it does not.

Classic Potato Fries

1/2 gallon peanut oil or canola oil
2 pounds russet potatoes, washed
    and cut into 1/4-inch-thick fries

Salt
Freshly ground black pepper

Preheat the oil in a large skillet or deep fryer to 300 degrees F.

Rinse the fries in a bowl of cold water and gently shake them with your hand to release some of the starches, then drain. Repeat this step. Pat the fries dry with paper towels. Place half of the dried potatoes in a fryer basket and submerge in the heated oil. Blanch them for 3 minutes, gently shaking the basket so that they do not stick together. Lift the basket from the oil and shake off the excess. Place the fries on a baking sheet lined with paper towels and spread them out. Cool the fries by placing them in the freezer while the other half is blanching. Chill the second half of the blanched fries in the freezer.

Increase the heat to 350 degrees F. Add the fries to the preheated oil and cook them for 2 to 3 minutes, or until golden brown and crispy. Transfer the fries to paper towels. Season to taste with salt and pepper. Allow to cool slightly before eating.

Original Simmons

MAKES 4 SANDWICHES

A sandwich that started out as a Magnolias' "dishwasher special" has become a local legend. I promptly named it to honor the line cooks, now chefs—James and Landice Simmons—who came up with the winning combination. The Original Simmons is a menu favorite and has even led to a casual food franchise put together by two of our former waiters. The sandwich is often duplicated now, but our original is still the best.

4 boneless, skinless chicken breasts, fried
   (see page 153 for how to fry chicken)
1 1/2 cups Pimiento Cheese (page 49)
4 fresh potato rolls
Sriracha Mayo (recipe follows)
Bread and Butter Pickles (page 16)
Jalapeño-Peach Coleslaw (page 112)

Preheat the oven to 300 degrees F.

On a baking sheet, top each fried chicken breast with 3 ounces of pimiento cheese and place in the oven to melt the cheese. Divide the buns in half and butter the inside of each half, then lightly toast the buns on a flattop or griddle. Spread 1 teaspoon of Sriracha mayo on the inside of each top and bottom bun. Arrange the chicken on the bottom bun and top with pickles and coleslaw. Serve immediately.

Sriracha Mayo

MAKES 1 CUP

1 cup Duke's mayonnaise
5 tablespoons Sriracha sauce
Juice from 1 lime

1/2 teaspoon kosher salt
1/4 teaspoon chopped or granulated garlic

In a small mixing bowl, combine all the ingredients and mix well. Store in an airtight container and refrigerate for up to 2 weeks.

continued »

Jalapeño-Peach Coleslaw

Did I mention that I am a coleslaw aficionado? If a place has coleslaw on the menu, I always give it a try. I have had some really good coleslaw and some, well, not so good. I'm more inclined to vinegar-based slaw, but the majority of recipes you find down South are creamy. This one uses a combination of both.

This recipe represents one of the things you come up with on the fly one day, thinking about, "What can I make for a special?" At the time it came to me, we had coleslaw on the menu with our fish tacos. But I needed something to accompany a fried chicken sandwich. It was peach season, so we sliced up a bunch of fresh peaches and a couple of jalapeños and added it to the slaw. A good start, but we were still missing something. We put a couple of ladles of the peach chutney that we serve with the Down South Egg Roll into the mix to cool it off a little bit. I think we ended up with a home run! It's now been on Magnolias' menu for about twenty years.

1 head cabbage, thinly sliced
1 small red onion, thinly sliced
2 small jalapeños, seeded and minced
2 green onions, thinly sliced
1 carrot, peeled and shredded
3 peaches, peeled and thinly sliced
1/2 cup Duke's mayonnaise
2 tablespoons spicy brown mustard

1 tablespoon apple cider vinegar
1 to 4 teaspoons granulated sugar
  (1 if using peach chutney, 4 if not)
1/4 teaspoon celery seed
1/4 teaspoon cumin
Pinch freshly ground black pepper
1/3 cup Peach Chutney (optional, page 47)

In a mixing bowl, combine the cabbage, red onion, jalapeños, green onions, carrot, and peaches.

In a separate mixing bowl, combine the mayonnaise, mustard, vinegar, sugar, celery seed, cumin, and pepper and mix well until the sugar has dissolved. Add the chutney, mixing well.

Combine the cabbage mixture with the dressing and mix together until well incorporated.

Note: The recipe calls for a head of fresh green cabbage, but you can substitute a bag of pre-shredded coleslaw mix if you need to save some time. When adding the coleslaw dressing to the vegetables, start by adding 1/4 cup of dressing, toss, and continue adding until you reach the desired level of creaminess. You probably will not need to use the entire batch of dressing.

FISH
and
SHELLFISH

Spicy Shrimp and Sausage with Creamy White Grits and Tasso Gravy

SERVES 8

While a traditional staple of Southern pantries, grits weren't typically served for dinner at fine-dining restaurants—until Magnolias. We were one of the first restaurants to elevate grits from the breakfast shift. This grits dish has been on our dinner menu since opening night—for more than thirty years. It's been served to queens, kings, and presidents, and today it turns up on local tables morning, noon, and night.

¾ pound uncooked spicy Italian sausage
1 tablespoon olive oil
2 pounds medium or large peeled
 and deveined shrimp
1½ cups Chicken Broth (page 19), divided

Tasso Gravy (page 116)
2 tablespoons finely chopped
 fresh parsley, divided
Creamy White Grits (page 116)

Preheat the oven to 400 degrees F.

Put the Italian sausage on a baking sheet. Bake on the top rack of the oven for 10 to 15 minutes, or until the sausage is firm and its juices run clear. Allow to cool before cutting into small bite-size pieces.

In a heavy-bottom frying pan over medium heat, heat the olive oil. Add the cooked sausage and sauté for 2 minutes to brown slightly. Add the shrimp and cook until they begin to turn pink—no longer than 1 minute. Add 1 cup of chicken broth to deglaze the pan. Add the tasso gravy and 1 tablespoon of parsley. Bring to a boil and let simmer for 1 minute. Use the remaining ½ cup chicken broth if the gravy needs to be thinned.

Divide the hot grits among 8 bowls and spoon the shrimp and sausage mixture over the grits. Sprinkle with the remaining 1 tablespoon of parsley and serve immediately.

continued »

Tasso Gravy

Tasso is cured pork (butt or shoulder) that's been heavily spiced and smoked. It's too much on its own, but added as a flavoring, sautéed with a little olive oil or butter, it really transports the spices off the ham and into a sauce or gravy like this one.

4 tablespoons unsalted butter
1/2 cup sliced tasso ham, cut in 1-inch strips
1/2 cup flour
4 cups Chicken Broth (page 19), divided

2 tablespoons finely chopped fresh parsley
Salt
White pepper

In a heavy-bottom saucepan over low heat, melt the butter. Add the tasso and sauté for 1 minute, browning slightly. Add the flour and make a roux, whisking until well combined.

Continue to cook over low heat for 5 minutes, whisking frequently, until the roux develops a nutty aroma. Turn the heat up to medium and gradually add 2 cups of the chicken broth, whisking vigorously. Keep whisking constantly until the broth begins to thicken and is smooth. Gradually add the remaining 2 cups of broth, whisking constantly until the broth thickens into gravy. Reduce the heat and simmer over low heat for 15 minutes to cook out the starchy flavor. Add the parsley. Simmer for another 5 minutes. Season to taste with salt and white pepper.

Creamy White Grits

12 cups Chicken Broth (page 19)
4 1/2 cups coarse stone-ground white grits
1 cup heavy (whipping) cream

Salt
White pepper

In a heavy-bottom stockpot or large saucepan, bring the chicken broth to a boil. Slowly pour in the grits, stirring constantly. Reduce the heat to low and continue to stir so that the grits do not settle to the bottom and scorch. In about 5 minutes, the grits will plump up and become a thick mass.

Continue to cook the grits for 20 to 25 minutes while stirring frequently. The grits should have absorbed all of the chicken broth and become soft. Add the heavy cream and cook for another 10 minutes, stirring frequently. The grits should have a thick consistency and be creamy like oatmeal. Season to taste with salt and white pepper. Keep warm over low heat until ready to serve. If the grits become too thick, add warm chicken broth or water to thin them down.

Atlantic Blue Crabs

You can find blue crabs all along the East Coast of the United States, from the beaches to the Intercoastal Waterway. Living in Charleston for more than twenty years, I've found that crabbing is a great way to spend a beautiful day. If you prefer the easy route and want to buy some live blue crabs, they come by the third, half, and whole bushel. Males—called Jimmies—are the ones you want to look for because they're bigger and meatier, but they often only sell bushels of mixed. If you are not cooking the crabs right away, you want to keep them moist, but don't throw them in a cooler of water; they'll use up the oxygen and die. Instead, cover them with a water-soaked newspaper and keep them cool, but not submerged.

About every coastal area will have a local spice mix that's used for seafood boils. Otherwise, Old Bay Seasoning is readily available and always a great standby. Be sure to serve these crabs with melted butter! A batch of these always makes for a wonderful evening of crab picking and conversation with friends and family.

2 cups steaming liquid (water, beer, or
  white vinegar, or a mixture of all three)
1/3 bushel large blue crabs
1 cup local spice blend or Old Bay Seasoning
1/2 pound butter, melted

SPECIAL EQUIPMENT
heavy rubber gloves
long tongs
steam pot with lid and strainer

In a large pot or steamer, pour in enough liquid to be 1 inch deep. Place the pot over high heat and bring to a boil. Place the live crabs in the steamer basket a few at a time and sprinkle the spice blend liberally over them. Add a few more crabs, then spice, repeating until the steamer basket is full. Place the basket in the pot and attach the lid firmly. Be sure to try to keep the crabs above the liquid level so that they will steam and not boil. Allow the crabs to steam for 18 to 20 minutes for large crabs and 16 to 18 for smaller ones. Remove from the heat and carefully take off the lid. Allow for some of the steam to escape before you pull out the steamer basket. Pour onto a table or platter and allow the crabs to cool down for about 5 minutes before picking.

Sautéed Grouper with Artichokes, Sautéed Spinach, Creamy Crab Meat, and Lemon and Leek Butter

SERVES 4

Grouper has to be one of my favorite Lowcountry fish to eat. It's one of the best bottom fish in the local offshore waters—highly protected and available only during certain times of the year. When you see grouper on a menu, order it! Grouper goes by many names like "black," "gag," "yellowedge," and "red." Any one of the above will do fine for this dish.

Artichokes (recipe follows)
Sautéed Spinach (page 122)
Creamy Crab Meat (page 122)
Lemon and Leek Butter (page 123)
Fried Leeks (page 123)

4 tablespoons light olive oil
4 (4- to 5-ounce) grouper fillets
1 teaspoon coarse sea salt
$\frac{1}{2}$ teaspoon white pepper
$\frac{1}{2}$ cup all-purpose flour

Preheat the oven to 300 degrees F.

Prepare the artichokes, spinach, creamy crab meat, lemon and leek butter, and fried leeks. Keep warm.

In a heavy-bottom, ovenproof frying pan, heat the olive oil until almost smoking. Season the fillets with the salt and white pepper and lightly dust in flour; pat off the excess. Gently place the fillets in the oil. Cook them for 2 to 3 minutes, lifting the fillets occasionally to let the oil help cook the fish evenly. Gently flip

and cook the opposite side for an additional 2 to 3 minutes, or until cooked through and the inner flesh of the fillet is white in color with no translucency.

Divide the spinach among 4 warmed plates. Place a fillet of grouper on top of the spinach. Top with the artichokes and then the creamy crab meat. Spoon a few tablespoons of the lemon and leek butter around the spinach and a little over the crab meat. Garnish with fried leeks. Serve immediately.

Artichokes

SERVES 4

2 quarts water
2 tablespoons light olive oil
1 tablespoon salt

1 lemon
2 fresh artichokes

continued »

In a nonreactive (nonaluminum) pot, combine the water, olive oil, and salt. Zest the lemon and reserve both the lemon and the zest. Cut the lemon in half, squeeze the juice into the water, and put the lemon halves into the water also. Pare the artichokes down to the bottom half, removing the leaves and keeping the choke intact with the artichoke bottom. Immediately put the artichokes in the water. Over medium-high heat, bring the artichokes to a simmer and allow to simmer for 20 to 25 minutes. Remove the pot from the heat and let the artichokes cook in the cooking liquid, about 20 minutes to finish cooking.

Remove the artichokes from the water and ease the choke out with your thumb and discard. Return the artichokes to the cooking liquid.

When ready to use, drain the artichokes. Slice each artichoke vertically into 1/4-inch-thick slices.

Sautéed Spinach

SERVES 4

2 tablespoons butter
3 cups baby spinach leaves
Fine sea salt
White pepper

In a large frying pan, melt the butter. Add the spinach and cook over medium-low heat until just wilted. Season to taste with salt and white pepper. Drain and keep warm.

Creamy Crab Meat

MAKES 1 TO 1 1/2 CUPS

1/2 cup heavy (whipping) cream
1/2 pound lump crab meat, picked over for shell and drained of any liquid

1 tablespoon minced fresh chives
Fine sea salt
White pepper

In a small saucepan over medium-high heat, reduce the cream by half. Add the crab meat and chives. Gently fold them together to warm the crab meat. Season to taste with salt and white pepper. Keep warm.

Lemon and Leek Butter

12 tablespoons (1 1/2 sticks)
    unsalted butter, divided
1 1/2 cups leeks (white part only), washed
    and drained well, cut into 1/4-inch dice
1 tablespoon white wine

1/4 cup heavy cream
1 teaspoon lemon zest
1/4 cup warm water, as needed
Fine sea salt
Pinch white pepper

Melt 4 tablespoons of butter in a saucepan. Add the leeks and cook them for 2 to 3 minutes, or until they have softened. Add the white wine, cook about 30 seconds, then add the cream and reduce by one-third. Add the lemon zest, then gradually whisk in the remaining 8 tablespoons of butter in small amounts over low heat. Be careful: If the sauce gets too hot, it may separate. The sauce is also at risk if it gets too cold so keep it at approximately 120 degrees F at all times. When all of the butter is incorporated and melted, the sauce will be thick and creamy. If too thick, adjust the consistency with up to 1/4 cup warm water. Season with salt and white pepper to taste. Keep warm.

Fried Leeks

2 cups oil
1 leek (white and green parts), top
    removed and julienned

In a frying pan, heat the oil to 350 degrees F. Fry the leek until crispy, about 3 to 4 minutes. Remove from the oil and place on a paper towel to drain off any excess oil.

Shellfish over Grits

Shellfish over Grits is yet another Magnolias classic. It's a twist on the everyday shrimp and grits, with lobster, scallops, and lobster sauce adding a touch of sophistication. Think of this elegant recipe for a special-occasion seated dinner—even New Year's Eve. The recipe looks intimidating, but it's well worth the effort, and you and your guests will love it. Once you get the stock made, the dish comes together rather quickly.

3 cups water
3 (1 1/4 pound) live Maine lobsters
3 tablespoons butter
3 tablespoons minced shallots
1 1/2 pounds large sea scallops

1 1/2 pounds large shrimp,
    peeled and deveined
3 tablespoons thinly sliced fresh basil, divided
Lobster Stock (page 126)
Lobster Sauce (page 126)
Creamy White Grits (page 116)

In a large pot with a tight-fitting lid, bring the water to a boil. Place the lobsters in the pot, cover, and steam for 6 to 7 minutes.

While the lobsters steam, prepare an ice bath. Remove the lobsters from the pot and immerse them totally in the ice bath to cool. Reserve the pot and the steaming liquid. When the lobsters are cool enough to handle, remove the claws and tails over the pot in order to catch all of the juices. Reserve the liquid in the pot for later use.

Using the back of a heavy spoon, lightly tap the claws on the side to crack the shells. Remove the claw meat, leaving as much intact as possible. Lay the tails on their sides and lightly tap to crack the shells. Remove the tail meat, leaving as much intact as possible. Remove the intestinal tracts along the back of the tail meat and discard. Reserve all of the shells for making lobster stock. Transfer the lobster meat to a bowl and refrigerate until ready to use.

Prepare the lobster stock, lobster sauce, and creamy white grits.

In a large pot, melt the butter without browning it. Add the shallots and cook until translucent, about 2 to 3 minutes. Add the sea scallops and the shrimp. Cook over low heat for 2 to 3 minutes, until the scallops are firm but a little translucent in the center and the shrimp are pink. Be careful not to overcook. Add the lobster meat and 2 tablespoons of basil and sauté until warm. Add the lobster sauce and heat until warmed throughout.

Divide the grits among 8 bowls. Top the grits with the shellfish. Spoon the lobster sauce over the shellfish and garnish with the remaining tablespoon of basil. Serve immediately.

continued »

Lobster Stock

Reserved cooking liquid of lobsters
4 tablespoons light olive oil
3/4 cup chopped onion
3/4 cup chopped celery
1/2 cup chopped carrot
2 garlic cloves, smashed
3 fresh tarragon sprigs

6 leaves fresh basil
2 bay leaves
4 black peppercorns, crushed
1 teaspoon fine sea salt
Reserved lobster shells
1 (6-ounce) can tomato paste

Combine the reserved liquid from cooking the lobsters with water to make 8 cups total of liquid. Set aside.

In a large, heavy-bottom pot, heat the oil and add the onion, celery, and carrot. Cook over low heat until the vegetables are soft, but not caramelized. Add the garlic, tarragon, basil, bay leaves, peppercorns, and salt. Cook for 1 minute. Add the lobster shells. Crush the bodies with a spoon or the end of a mallet to release the juices from the body cavity. Add the tomato paste and stir to coat the shells. Continue to cook until liquid has been reduced by half and the mixture is pasty.

Add the water and liquid from cooking the lobsters and bring slowly to a simmer. Remove any foam that may rise to the top and discard. Simmer for 35 minutes.

When cool enough to handle, strain the stock through a fine sieve, pressing the solids to remove the maximum amount of stock. Transfer the stock to a saucepan, bring to a boil, and reduce it to 2 cups to concentrate the flavor. Cool to room temperature. Store in an airtight container for 3 to 4 days in the refrigerator or up to 6 months in the freezer.

Lobster Sauce

3 tablespoons unsalted butter, divided
1/4 cup all-purpose flour
2 cups Lobster Stock (above), divided
1/2 cup heavy cream

1 tablespoon brandy
Fine sea salt
White pepper
Cayenne pepper

In a saucepan, melt 2 tablespoons of butter without browning it. Stir in the flour and cook over low heat for 2 minutes. Add 1 cup of the lobster stock and whisk vigorously to make a smooth paste. Add the remaining cup of stock and whisk until smooth. Add the cream and brandy and simmer slowly over low heat for 10 to 15 minutes, whisking occasionally. Add the remaining tablespoon of butter. Season to taste with salt, white pepper and cayenne pepper. Remove from heat, allow to cool slightly, and cover with plastic wrap to prevent a skin from forming over the sauce.

Coriander Seared Tuna with Herb Potato Cakes, Sautéed Escarole, and Jalapeño-Mango Vinaigrette

SERVES 4

This recipe has been one of Magnolias' favorite tuna dishes on the menu over the years. The coriander crust gives it the spice and the jalapeño-mango vinaigrette has both sweetness and heat that complement the dish. Make sure to rub the fish with the coriander rub a couple of hours ahead of time.

4 (5- to 6-ounce) tuna fillets
4 tablespoons Coriander Rub (recipe follows)
Herb Potato Cakes (page 128)

Sautéed Escarole (page 129)
Jalapeño-Mango Vinaigrette (page 129)
2 tablespoons light olive oil

Rub the tuna fillets with the coriander rub on all sides. Cover and refrigerate for at least 3 hours, or overnight.

Prepare the potato cakes, escarole, and jalapeño-mango vinaigrette.

In a heavy-bottom saucepan over medium-high heat, heat the olive oil. Carefully place the tuna fillets in the oil and sear until a crust forms, 2 to 3 minutes. Gently turn them over and sauté for 2 1/2 to 3 minutes for medium rare.

In the center of the plates, place the potato cakes and add some of the cooked escarole around them. Top with the tuna and spoon some of the vinaigrette over and around it. Serve immediately.

Coriander Rub

MAKES 1/2 CUP

5 tablespoons coriander seeds
1 tablespoon ground ginger
2 tablespoons freshly ground black pepper

1/4 teaspoon cayenne pepper
2 tablespoons coarse sea salt
1/2 cup light olive oil

Preheat the oven to 350 degrees F.

Place the coriander seeds on a baking sheet with raised sides and cook in the oven for 5 minutes to toast the seeds and intensify the coriander flavor. Remove and allow the coriander to cool completely. Transfer the seeds to a spice grinder and pulse until they are pulverized, but not quite a powder. In a small bowl, combine the coriander, ginger, black pepper, cayenne pepper, sea salt, and olive oil and mix well to combine. Reserve until ready to use.

continued »

Herb Potato Cakes

2 cups peeled russet potatoes,
   cut into equal-size pieces
3 cups water
1 1/2 teaspoons salt, divided
2 tablespoons butter
1/4 cup finely diced onion
1 teaspoon minced garlic

2 tablespoons heavy (whipping) cream
1/8 teaspoon white pepper
1 tablespoon minced fresh parsley
1/2 cup panko breadcrumbs,
   plus more for dusting
1/4 cup light olive oil

In a saucepan over medium heat, bring the potatoes, water, and 1 teaspoon salt to a boil and cook for 18 to 20 minutes, or until the potatoes are tender. Drain off the water and return the pan to the heat for 1 minute, stirring constantly to steam-dry the potatoes. (This helps remove some of the excessive moisture.)

In a small saucepan, melt the butter. Add the onion and garlic and cook for 1 minute without browning. Add the cream, remaining 1/2 teaspoon of salt, and the white pepper and stir well. Pour into the cooked potato mixture and mix gently to combine. Add the parsley and the breadcrumbs, allowing everything to absorb. Shape into 1/2-cup size cakes that are at least 1 1/4 inches thick. Dust with additional panko.

In a heavy-bottom frying pan over medium-high heat, heat the olive oil. Sauté the potato cakes about 4 to 5 minutes per side, until golden on both sides and heated through. If not using the cakes right away, place them in an oven preheated to 200 degrees F to keep warm.

Sautéed Escarole

2 tablespoons light olive oil
6 cups roughly chopped escarole,
  washed and dried

1 teaspoon minced garlic
Salt
Freshly ground black pepper

In a large, heavy-bottom frying pan over medium heat, heat the oil. Add the escarole and toss gently until it begins to wilt. Add the garlic and continue to cook for 2 minutes. Season with salt and pepper to taste. Keep warm.

Jalapeño-Mango Vinaigrette

2 tablespoons Dijon mustard
2 tablespoons apple cider vinegar
1/4 cup fresh lemon juice
1 cup light olive oil
2 tablespoons chopped chives

1 teaspoon minced garlic
1 tablespoon minced jalapeño
3/4 cup diced mango
1/4 teaspoon freshly ground black pepper

In a bowl, whisk together the mustard, vinegar, and lemon juice. Add the olive oil very slowly in a steady stream, whisking vigorously until the oil is incorporated. Add the chives, garlic, jalapeño, mango, and black pepper and stir to combine. Reserve at room temperature.

Iron-Skillet Crispy Flounder with Lemon-Caper Aioli

SERVES 2

Garibaldi's (Italian) restaurant in Charleston's market area might have been the first place I tried whole-fried flounder. They've sadly long-since shuttered, but Magnolias still carries the torch for this dish, spotlighting a popular, plentiful Lowcountry fish. Our recipe allows the flounder's flavor to shine with a simple accompaniment of aioli.

If you don't have the opportunity to go fishing, try to have your seafood guy pick out a 1 to 1 1/2-pound fish at the market. For the best result, use a large, heavy-bottom cast-iron pan and fill it with oil 1 inch up the side, or place the fish one at a time in a turkey fryer; just handle it carefully. It's a dish best cooked outside.

8 cups peanut oil or canola oil

2 cups all-purpose flour

2 tablespoons fine sea salt, plus more for seasoning

1 tablespoon white pepper, plus more for seasoning

1 (1- to 1 1/2- pound) whole flounder, head off, cleaned, and scaled

Lemon-Caper Aioli (recipe follows)

In a large skillet, deep fryer, or turkey fryer basket, preheat the oil to 340 degrees F.

Mix the flour, salt, and white pepper together on a baking sheet with raised edges that is a little bigger than the flounder. Set aside.

With the dark side of the flounder up, use a sharp knife to score the flesh just to the bone with 1-inch parallel cuts at an angle. Be careful not to cut through the bone. Continue to the tail end. Rotate the flounder 90 degrees and score again at an angle to make diamonds. Flip the flounder over and repeat this process on the lighter side.

Season the fish with salt and pepper to taste before dredging it in the seasoned flour. Bend the flounder gently to get some of the seasoning in the areas where it was scored. Dredge it in the seasoned flour again and be sure that the exposed flesh of the flounder is coated in the flour.

Gently place the flounder in the heated oil, dark-side down first. Watch over it constantly to control the heat. To prevent burning and allow the fish to cook evenly, give it an occasional lift with a pair of tongs or a fish spatula to make sure that there is oil in between the flounder and the skillet. Fry it for 5 to 6 minutes per side, or until it is golden brown and no translucent flesh is apparent in the cuts. Gently turn the flounder over and cook for an additional 3 to 4 minutes. Remove the fish from the skillet, place it on several paper towels, and allow it to cool for a few minutes. Serve the fish on a platter, accompanied by the lemon-caper aioli.

Lemon-Caper Aioli

1/2 cup Duke's mayonnaise
2 tablespoons minced capers
1 tablespoon fresh lemon juice

1 teaspoon chopped fresh parsley
Salt
White pepper

In a small mixing bowl, combine the mayonnaise, capers, lemon juice, and parsley and mix well. Season to taste with salt and white pepper.

Lowcountry Bouillabaisse

This recipe is Magnolias' version of a classic bouillabaisse. Local fish and shellfish, sweet corn, spicy potlikker, and tasso give the dish layers of Southern flavor.

Potlikker (recipe follows), divided
3 tablespoons light olive oil
3/4 cup Cooked Yellow Corn
    Kernels (page 184)
1/4 cup diced red bell peppers,
    cut in 1/4-inch dice
1/4 cup diced celery, cut in 1/4-inch dice
1/4 cup red onion, cut in 1/4-inch dice
1/4 cup diced tasso ham, cut in 1/4-inch dice
1 dozen clams, scrubbed and washed well

1 cup white wine
18 mussels, scrubbed and debearded
18 large shrimp, peeled and deveined
1 pound whitefish, such as grouper
    or snapper, cut in 1-inch pieces
1 cup diced cooked new potatoes, skin on
2 tablespoons minced fresh parsley, divided
1 teaspoon sea salt
1 teaspoon freshly ground black pepper
Croutons (page 134)

Prepare the potlikker and set aside.

In a large saucepan with a lid, heat the olive oil over medium-high heat. Add the corn, peppers, celery, red onion, and tasso ham. Cook for 3 to 4 minutes, stirring frequently, until the vegetables soften and the tasso spices are released. Add the clams and stir for another 2 minutes to start the cooking process. Add the white wine and 1 cup of potlikker. Increase the heat to high and cover and allow to steam for 6 to 7 minutes, then reduce the heat to medium. Carefully remove the lid and add the mussels, shrimp, fish, and potatoes. Add enough potlikker to cover the surface of the shellfish. Cover and poach for 6 to 8 minutes, or until the fish and shrimp are cooked through and the mussels are open; an occasional stir may be necessary. Add 1 tablespoon of parsley and the salt and pepper.

Divide the seafood equally among 6 large bowls. Ladle some of the potlikker with the vegetables and tasso over it. Sprinkle with the remaining 1 tablespoon of parsley, place a crouton on each dish, and serve immediately.

Potlikker

2 tablespoons light olive oil
1/2 cup yellow corn kernels
2 tablespoons finely chopped jalapeño
2 tablespoons roughly chopped garlic
4 fresh thyme sprigs
2 bay leaves
1 teaspoon red chili flakes

2 cups white wine
6 cups clam juice
6 cups tomato juice
2 cups water
Pinch saffron threads
Fine sea salt
Freshly ground black pepper

continued »

In a heavy-bottom soup pot over medium heat, heat the olive oil. Add the corn, jalapeño, garlic, thyme sprigs, bay leaves, and chili flakes; cook for 1 minute without browning. Add the white wine and cook for 3 minutes. Add the clam juice, tomato juice, and water, then increase the heat to medium-high and bring to a boil. Reduce to a simmer, then remove and discard any foam that may appear. Add the saffron, then reduce the potlikker by one-third to one-half of its volume. Season to taste with salt and pepper. Strain through a sieve. Reserve warm for immediate use or cool to room temperature, transfer to a storage container, cover, and refrigerate for up to 1 week.

Croutons

MAKES 4 SERVINGS

4 bias–cut French baguette
    slices, ¼-inch thick
2 tablespoons butter

Spread the baguette slices with the butter and toast under a broiler or on a grill until golden and crispy.

Fire-Roasted Cedar-Planked Salmon with Dill-Shallot Compound Butter

SERVES 10 TO 12

Preparing this dish is an experience best enjoyed on weekends and holidays when it's starting to get cold outside. My family likes to cook a planked salmon side for Christmas every year while we sit around the fire pit and celebrate the season.

A few years back, I found a hack to simplify the setup: Go to your local hardware store and buy a cedar plank, ten small nails, some baling wire, and two hanging plant holders. The hanging plant holders have two pointed ends and a half circle that holds the potted plant. Cut that circle off with a hacksaw and you end up with a Y-shaped metal pole. Use the modified Y end to stick into the ground, and use the two point ends of each pole to hold the cedar plank.

Place the planked fish over the fire and, halfway through cooking, invert the salmon so that it's over the flame. Make sure the fish is far enough away that the herbs on top of it don't burn.

continued »

1 (2 1/2– to 3–pound) salmon fillet
   with the skin attached
1/4 cup coarse sea salt, divided
2 tablespoons freshly ground black pepper
1 bunch fresh rosemary sprigs
1 bunch fresh thyme sprigs
Creamy White Grits (page 116)
Dill–Shallot Compound Butter (recipe follows)

SPECIAL EQUIPMENT
Seasoned oak, hickory, or choice
   of hardwood for the fire
1 cedar plank, 8 inches wide
   and at least 5 feet long
10 small nails or screws
Metal wire
1 pair wire cutters

Start the fire a couple of hours ahead of time so that you have a bed of coals as wide as the fillet is long. Prepare the plank by toasting one side over the hot coals until it begins to blacken slightly. Allow the cedar to cool. Place the plank so that it rests with a support on either end with the toasted side up. Sprinkle it with about 1/8 cup coarse sea salt. Once cool, tap 5 nails down the lengthwise edge of the plank. Repeat with the other nails on the other lengthwise edge of the plank.

Place the salmon fillet on the plank skin-side down. Season the top side of the salmon with the remaining salt and pepper. Lay the rosemary and thyme sprigs lengthwise on the fillet. Starting at the large end of the fillet, twist the wire around the top nail a time or two until you are sure that it will hold. Wrap the wire between the top and bottom nail. The wire should be fairly tight, but not so tight that it slices through the tender flesh of the salmon. Continue from the bottom nail to the next top nail, until the length of the salmon

is secure, and then twist the wire around the last nail on the tail side. Trim off any excess wire.

Arrange the plank supports near the fire. Place the plank, skin-side down, 15 to 20 inches above the hot coals. It is best that the salmon is roasted slowly at first. Try not to scorch the herbs before the salmon cooks. The longer the salmon cooks, the better the roasted flavor. The oils of the salmon will be released and the flesh of the salmon should caramelize slightly. This imparts a great flavor and texture to the salmon.

Roast the salmon for 20 minutes, or until the thicker section of the fillet feels firm to the touch. Rotate the salmon so the flesh is facing the fire and cook for additional 5 minutes. The cooking time will vary due to the heat of the fire and the distance the salmon is kept from the fire.

When finished, unwrap the wire from the nails and serve the salmon on the plank with the grits and dill-shallot compound butter.

Dill-Shallot Compound Butter

MAKES 1/2 CUP

1/2 pound unsalted butter, room temperature
1/4 cup minced shallots
2 tablespoons chopped fresh dill or
   1 tablespoon dried dill weed

1 teaspoon coarse sea salt
1/2 teaspoon freshly ground black pepper

In a bowl, mix the softened butter with the shallots, dill, salt, and pepper.

Parmesan-Crusted Flounder with Carolina Jasmine Rice and Shrimp Pirloo, Sweet Corn, Tomato, and Asparagus Salad, and Citrus Beurre Blanc

SERVES 4

This dish has been a customer favorite for many years. When fresh local flounder hasn't been available, I've tried a few times to slip this offering off the menu, but customers raise a fuss and demand that we serve it even if we have to bring the flounder in from elsewhere. I am happy—and flattered—to oblige. There are several steps to this dish, but it's well worth the effort. If flounder isn't available, other options are halibut, snapper, grouper, or mahi-mahi.

2 cups Parmesan Crust (recipe follows)

1 1/2 pounds flounder fillets, about 6 ounces per person (check for bones)

4 tablespoons olive oil

Carolina Jasmine Rice (page 140)

Shrimp Pirloo (page 140)

Sweet Corn, Tomato, and Asparagus Salad (page 141)

Citrus Beurre Blanc (page 141)

1/2 pound jumbo lump crab meat (optional)

Pour the Parmesan crust mixture into a medium bowl and coat the flounder on all sides. Heat a skillet on the stovetop over medium heat (or bake flounder in a 300-degree F oven for 12 to 15 minutes on a baking sheet). Carefully add the olive oil to the pan and place the flounder good-side up in the pan. Cook for about 2 minutes, flip, and cook for another 3 minutes, or until done. You want a nice golden crust. Keep warm.

Divide the shrimp pirloo among 4 to 6 plates. Top with the Parmesan flounder. Divide the sweet corn, tomato, and asparagus salad evenly on top of the fillets. Ladle the citrus beurre blanc around the edge of the plate. Finish by sprinkling jumbo lump crab meat on top of the beurre blanc, if desired.

Parmesan Crust

MAKES 4 1/2 CUPS

1 1/4 cup grated Parmesan cheese

3 cups panko breadcrumbs

1/4 teaspoon granulated garlic

1/4 teaspoon granulated onion

1 teaspoon paprika

2 tablespoons olive oil

1 tablespoon chopped fresh parsley

Pinch coarse sea salt

Pinch freshly ground black pepper

continued »

In a food processor fitted with a metal blade, combine all the ingredients and pulse for 30 seconds. Store in an airtight container.

Carolina Jasmine Rice

MAKES 4 CUPS

2 cups jasmine rice
3 cups water

1 teaspoon sea salt

In a strainer, rinse the rice under cold water to remove some of the unwanted starch.

Combine the rice, water, and salt in a medium saucepot, cover with a lid, and bring slowly to a boil over medium-high heat. When you see steam trying to escape, reduce the heat to low and simmer for 12 to 15 minutes. It's best not to peek. When the rice is cooked and the lid removed, little steam holes should be present and all water should be absorbed. Let the rice rest for a minute or two, then fluff with a fork. Keep warm.

Shrimp Pirloo

SERVES 4

1 tablespoon butter
1/2 pound fresh shrimp (about 26 to 30), peeled and deveined (reserve shells for stock)
1/4 cup diced yellow onion
2 tablespoons diced red bell pepper
1 tablespoon diced celery
1 cup Lobster Stock (page 126) or Shrimp Stock (page 21)

1 cup heavy (whipping) cream
3 cups cooked Carolina Jasmine Rice (page 140)
1/4 cup Parmesan cheese
1 teaspoon coarse sea salt
1/2 teaspoon freshly ground black pepper
1/3 cup thinly sliced green onion

In a medium skillet over medium-high heat, melt the butter and sauté the shrimp, onion, bell pepper, and celery. Cook until the shrimp are pink. Add the stock and heavy cream. Reduce by one-third. Add the rice, Parmesan, salt, pepper, and green onion and cook until the rice is well coated. Remove from the heat and serve immediately.

Sweet Corn, Tomato, and Asparagus Salad

SERVES 4

1 tablespoon olive oil or unsalted butter
2 cups (¼-inch pieces) asparagus,
   blanched (about 20 spears)
1 cup fresh yellow corn kernels
1 cup cherry tomatoes, halved

2 stems fresh basil, leaves
   pulled and julienned
½ teaspoon coarse sea salt
½ teaspoon freshly ground black pepper

In a medium skillet over medium heat, heat the olive oil. Add the asparagus and sauté for 1 minute. Add the corn and cook for 30 seconds. Add the cherry tomato halves, basil, salt, and pepper, and cook until heated throughout. Keep warm.

Citrus Beurre Blanc

MAKES 2 CUPS

2 shallots, minced
1 cup dry white wine
2 tablespoons fresh lemon juice
¼ teaspoon black peppercorns
1 bay leaf

½ cup heavy (whipping) cream
1½ cups unsalted butter, cut
   into ½-inch pieces
Coarse sea salt
White pepper

Combine the shallots, wine, lemon juice, peppercorns and bay leaf in a nonreactive (nonaluminum) pan over high heat and reduce to 2 tablespoons. Add the cream to the reduction. Let it reduce by two-thirds, or until it starts to bubble. Turn the heat down to low and start adding the butter one piece at a time. (A little trick to help the sauce from breaking: When you whisk in the butter, whisk the first piece on the heat and the next one off the heat. Continue the rotation until the sauce is fully emulsified.) Remove from the heat, strain the sauce through a fine-mesh strainer to remove the spices, and adjust seasoning to taste. Keep in a warm place until ready to use.

Blackened Catfish with Pimiento Cheese Crust, Marsh Hen Yellow Grits, Succotash, and Tomato Butter

SERVES 4

This is an impressive way to cook up a simple catfish. The recipe pulls out all of the stops with the combination of pimiento cheese and tomato butter. Wow! Marsh Hen Mill on Edisto Island produces the best local grits around these parts. As always, cooking grits in chicken broth is the best way to add flavor.

4 (7- to 8-ounce) catfish fillets
1/2 cup Magnolias' Blackening Spice (page 27)
2 cups Marsh Hen Yellow Grits (recipe follows)
4 cups Succotash (page 184)

1 1/2 cups Tomato Butter (page 58)
2 tablespoons canola oil
8 ounces Pimiento Cheese (page 49), divided
2 tablespoons chopped fresh parsley

Preheat the oven to 350 degrees F.

Sprinkle the catfish with the blackening spice, covering the fillets on all sides. Prepare the grits, succotash, and tomato butter; keep warm.

In an oven-safe skillet large enough to hold all 4 fillets over medium-high heat, heat the oil. Once hot, carefully place the fish into the pan and cook the fish on both sides for 3 to 4 minutes per side. Remove the pan from the heat and top each fillet with 2 ounces of pimiento cheese. Place the pan in the oven and allow the cheese to melt for 3 to 5 minutes. Serve with grits, succotash, and tomato butter. Garnish with the parsley.

Marsh Hen Yellow Grits

MAKES 4 CUPS

3 cups Chicken Broth (page 19)
1 cup Marsh Hen yellow grits
1/3 cup heavy (whipping) cream

2 tablespoons butter
Salt
Freshly ground black pepper

In a heavy-bottom saucepan over high heat, bring the chicken broth to a boil. Slowly pour in the grits while stirring constantly. Reduce the heat to low and continue to stir so the grits don't settle to the bottom and scorch. Cook uncovered for 5 minutes more. The grits will thicken quickly. Add the heavy cream and butter and continue to cook for 15 minutes. Stir frequently and season with salt and pepper to taste. The grits will be creamy. Remove from heat and keep warm.

Sweet Chili–Rubbed Ahi Tuna with Pepper Jack and Hummus Spring Rolls, Creole Rémoulade, and Roasted Mango Salsa   SERVES 4

This is a variation of a wonderful tuna dish that was created by former Magnolias' chef Kelly Franz. The recipe has evolved over the years, and you'll still see it on our menu from time to time when fresh tuna is available.

4 (7- to 8-ounce) ahi-grade tuna fillets
Sweet Chili Rub (recipe follows)
1 cup Creole Rémoulade (recipe follows)

8 Pepper Jack and Hummus
   Spring Rolls (page 146)
2 cups Roasted Mango Salsa (page 146)

Fire the grill.

Evenly coat the tuna fillets with the sweet chili rub on both sides. Once the grill is hot, cook the tuna until it reaches desired doneness. The internal temperature should be between 120 degrees F and 130 degrees F for rare, 130 degrees F and 140 degrees F for medium-rare, and 140 degrees F and 150 degrees F for medium. (For ahi-grade tuna, it is best to serve it rare.)

Spoon 1/4 cup of rémoulade in the center of each plate and place two spring rolls on top of the rémoulade. Place a tuna fillet on top and garnish with the salsa.

Sweet Chili Rub   MAKES 1 1/2 CUPS

2 tablespoons paprika
1/2 tablespoon cumin
1 tablespoon granulated garlic
1 tablespoon granulated onion

3 tablespoons chili powder
1/2 tablespoon freshly ground black pepper
2 tablespoons brown sugar
1 tablespoon kosher salt

Mix all the ingredients well and store in an airtight container.

Creole Rémoulade   MAKES 1 1/4 CUPS

1 cup Duke's mayonnaise
1/4 cup buttermilk
1 tablespoon capers

1 teaspoon Magnolias' Blackening
   Spice (page 27)
1 teaspoon horseradish

continued »

In a small bowl, whisk all the ingredients together. Store in an airtight container and refrigerate for up to 1 week.

Pepper Jack and Hummus Spring Rolls

MAKES 8 SPRING ROLLS

2 cloves minced garlic
1 (19-ounce) can garbanzo beans
4 tablespoons lemon juice
2 tablespoons tahini
1 teaspoon salt

2 tablespoons olive oil
Freshly ground black pepper
1 1/2 cups shredded pepper Jack cheese
8 spring roll wrappers
3 cups canola oil

In a blender or food processor, blend the garlic, garbanzo beans, lemon juice, tahini, salt, olive oil, and black pepper until smooth. Pour into a medium bowl and add the shredded cheese; mix well.

Place the spring roll wrappers on the counter. Divide the hummus into 8 equal portions and place on top of each spring roll wrapper. Roll according to the instructions on the package, making sure to seal each spring roll tightly.

Preheat the canola oil to 350 degrees F in a large skillet or deep fryer. Once the oil is heated, fry the spring rolls according to the package instructions, for 4 to 5 minutes.

Roasted Mango Salsa

MAKES 2 CUPS

1/3 cup finely diced red onion
1 habanero or jalapeño, seeded and minced
3 ripe mangoes, diced
2 tablespoons olive oil, divided
2 teaspoons cumin
1 green bell pepper, seeded and diced

2 tablespoons lime juice
2 tomatoes, seeded and diced
1/3 cup fresh cilantro, chopped
Kosher salt
Freshly ground black pepper

Preheat the oven to 400 degrees F.

In a small bowl, toss the red onion, habanero pepper, and mangoes with 1 tablespoon of olive oil. Season with cumin and mix well. Spread on a small baking sheet and roast in the oven for 10 to 15 minutes. Remove from the oven and return to the bowl. Add the bell pepper, lime juice, and tomatoes and mix well. Add the remaining 1 tablespoon of olive oil and mix well. Allow to cool for 15 minutes before adding the cilantro. Mix well and season with salt and pepper to taste.

MEAT
and
POULTRY

Grilled Filet of Beef with Melted Pimiento Cheese, Herb Potato Cake, Grilled Tomatoes and Green Onions, and Madeira Sauce

SERVES 4

We serve our grilled beef filet on a warm plate with Madeira sauce, accompanied by vegetables and an herb potato cake, topped with house-made pimiento cheese. The combination of flavors, colors, and textures makes this an outstanding dish.

4 (6- to 8-ounce) filets of beef
2 tablespoons olive oil
Salt
Freshly ground black pepper
1 cup Pimiento Cheese (page 49)

Grilled Tomatoes and Green
    Onions (recipe follows)
Madeira Sauce (page 23)
Herb Potato Cakes (page 128)

Fire the grill. Brush the filets with olive oil and season to taste with salt and black pepper.

Place the filets on the hot grill, close the lid, and cook to just below the desired temperature. Depending on the intensity of the grill, a filet should cook 8 to 10 minutes per side to reach medium rare, with an internal temperature of 120 degrees F to 125 degrees F on a meat thermometer. (There are many factors to consider when determining how long to cook the filet: the thickness of the meat, the exact weight of the meat, and the heat of the grill. This is why a meat thermometer is helpful.)

When you get close to the desired temperature, remove the filets from the grill. Spread each filet with 2 or 3 tablespoons of pimiento cheese. Return the filets back to the grill, cheese side up, close the lid, and cook for another 2 to 3 minutes to allow the cheese to melt.

While the grill is still hot, prepare the tomatoes and green onions and set aside.

Spoon 3 ounces of Madeira sauce on the base of each of 4 large plates. Place a potato cake on one side and a scoop of grilled tomatoes and green onions on the other side. Add a filet and drizzle with additional Madeira sauce if desired.

Grilled Tomatoes and Green Onions

MAKES 4 SERVINGS

2 teaspoons olive oil
2 teaspoons minced garlic
$1/4$ teaspoon freshly ground black pepper
Salt

2 large tomatoes, cut across
    into slices $1/4$-inch thick
1 bunch green onions (6 to 8 pieces), roots
    and tips of green ends removed

In a bowl, make a marinade by mixing together the olive oil, garlic, pepper, and a dash of salt. Rub the marinade generously on the tomatoes and toss the green onions in the marinade. Grill the tomatoes for 3 to 4 minutes, gently turning once. Grill the green onions for 2 minutes and turn so that all sides are grilled.

Note: This marinade can be used for grilling a variety of vegetables such as bell peppers, asparagus, zucchini, yellow squash, yellow onions, corn on the cob, and eggplant.

Hickory-Smoked Pork Shoulder with Carolina Barbecue Sauce, Crackling Cream Biscuits, and Spicy Yellow Corn

SERVES 6 TO 8

Years ago, we took this recipe on the road to Chicago, where it won the Food Arts Magazine *BBQ Championship. I think it's still a winner! Rub your pork shoulder the day before cooking so that the spices really sink in and flavor the meat. On barbecue day, you will want to start cooking the pork early in the morning to have it ready by midafternoon.*

Dry Rub (recipe follows)
1 (6– to 7-pound) pork shoulder
Carolina Barbecue Sauce (page 152)

Crackling Cream Biscuits (page 152)
Spicy Yellow Corn (page 152)

Prepare the dry rub and coat the entire shoulder with three-fourths of the spice mixture and refrigerate for at least 1 hour, but preferably overnight. Reserve the remaining rub.

When ready to cook, preheat the grill or smoker to 265 degrees F using hickory chips or chunks that have been soaked ahead of time in water. Place the pork shoulder indirectly over the heat source and smoke it for 5 to 7 hours, or until the shoulder reaches an internal temperature of 185 degrees F for sliced pork shoulder and 190 degrees F for pulled pork shoulder. When using wood chips, add additional soaked chips every 40 minutes or so.

While the meat is cooking, prepare the barbecue sauce, biscuits, and corn.

When the shoulder has reached the desired temperature, remove the meat and allow it to rest for 10 to 15 minutes. Use immediately or cool to room temperature, cover, and refrigerate overnight.

If the pork had been refrigerated overnight, warm the pork in a small amount of the barbecue sauce to moisten and season it. Divide the pork among the plates and place 3 biscuits around it. Drizzle with more of the barbecue sauce and then sprinkle with the corn. Serve immediately.

Dry Rub

MAKES ½ CUP

2 teaspoons granulated garlic powder
1 teaspoon cumin
3 teaspoons freshly ground black pepper

½ teaspoon cayenne pepper
2 teaspoons granulated onion powder
2½ teaspoons salt

Mix all the ingredients together. Store in an airtight container until ready to use.

continued »

Carolina Barbecue Sauce

MAKES 3 CUPS

2 cups apple cider vinegar
1 1/2 cups apple cider
1 cup dark brown sugar
2 tablespoons yellow mustard seeds
2 tablespoons Dijon mustard

1/2 cup tomato paste
1/4 teaspoon salt
1/4 teaspoon freshly ground black pepper
2 smoked pork neck bones or ham hocks

In a heavy-bottom saucepan over medium heat, combine all the ingredients and allow to cook slowly for 30 to 40 minutes, or until the sauce thickens. Remove any foam that may appear on the surface of the sauce as it cooks. Check the seasoning. Remove the neck bones and allow the sauce to cool to room temperature. Check the seasoning and use immediately or transfer to a storage container, cool to room temperature, cover, and refrigerate for up to 2 weeks.

Crackling Cream Biscuits

MAKES 24 (1-INCH) BISCUITS

2 1/2 cups White Lily self-rising
   flour, plus more for flouring
2 cups heavy (whipping) cream, divided

4 tablespoons Country Ham
   Cracklings (page 52), divided
2 tablespoons coarse sea salt
3 tablespoons melted butter

Preheat the oven to 400 degrees F.

Put the flour in a mixing bowl. Pour 1 1/2 cups of cream into the flour until it starts to come together into a wet sticky dough. Add 2 tablespoons of ham cracklings and work together for a minute or so. Place on a lightly floured surface and press or roll the dough out to less than 1/2-inch thick. Brush the top of the biscuit dough with the remaining 1/2 cup of cream. This is to help hold the cracklings and salt on the biscuits after baking. Sprinkle the remaining 2 tablespoons of ham cracklings and the sea salt on the top of the dough and gently press down. Cut the biscuits with a 1-inch biscuit cutter. Place on an ungreased baking sheet and bake for 8 to 10 minutes, or until golden. Remove from the oven, brush with the melted butter, and serve immediately.

Spicy Yellow Corn

MAKES 2 1/2 CUPS

1 tablespoon light olive oil
2 cups fresh corn kernels
2 tablespoons Country Ham
   Cracklings (page 52)
Dry Rub (page 151)

Heat the oil in a medium-size saucepan and add the corn kernels. Allow the kernels to caramelize over medium heat. Add the cracklings and season to taste with the dry rub.

Buttermilk Fried Chicken

SERVES 6 TO 8

Family traditions run deep in the South. Good, honest fried chicken is one of them. Good fried chicken is difficult to cook at a busy restaurant because it takes a while to cook. But if you love fried chicken the way I do, you'll understand that it's worth the wait. In my family, fried chicken was our regular Sunday supper. The meal included mashed potatoes, biscuits, and gravy. Other side dishes would come and go depending on the season, but the rest always stayed the same.

Some home cooks I know like to use deep-fat fryers, and some won't even cook fried chicken unless they can use a heavy cast-iron skillet—preferably one that's been handed down a generation or two. My mom used to have an electric skillet that had two prongs; you plugged a black cloth cord into the pan. It had an adjustable thermostat on the cord and a semi-square-shaped lid. I wonder whatever happened to that pan!

Is a lid critical when cooking fried chicken to get that golden crispy texture? Mom said, "Yes." She would cook the chicken for about 30 minutes at 3 different temperatures. She would begin frying the chicken on high heat for about 5 minutes. Then, she would slow-fry with the lid on, and finish by removing the lid for the last couple of minutes to crisp the chicken. She strained off most of the grease and made her whitewash milk gravy in the skillet. It seems like only yesterday that Mom was in the kitchen frying up a batch of Sunday chicken.

Today in my own home, we still have to cook two chickens to feed the four of us and we're equally divided between the white meat and dark meat lovers. I hope you'll try this recipe and start your own fried chicken tradition!

2 (3 1/2-pound) kosher or air-chilled chickens, cut up
1 cup Texas Pete hot sauce
2 cups buttermilk
6 cups White Lily self-rising flour
2 tablespoons coarse sea salt

1 teaspoon garlic powder
2 teaspoons freshly ground black pepper
1 teaspoon cayenne pepper
1/2 teaspoon white pepper
Lard, peanut oil, or safflower oil

In a large plastic storage bag or container, cover the cold chicken with Texas Pete and buttermilk and allow to sit overnight, or a few hours at minimum. In a shallow pan or brown paper bag, mix together the flour, salt, garlic powder, black pepper, cayenne pepper, and white pepper. Remove the cold chicken from the buttermilk a piece at a time and place it in the bag. Shake the bag to coat the chicken well, remove, and shake off any excess flour.

Fill a large skillet about halfway with your choice of fat (I like using lard best) and heat on high. When the lard is melted or the oil is 325 degrees F, add the chicken, skin-side down. If you're frying different-size pieces, start with the bigger ones. Fried chicken is best started on high heat because the temperature of the oil will drop as cold pieces of chicken are added to the pan. When the skillet is full, turn the heat down to medium and fry the chicken until just golden brown and crispy, then turn and fry the other side until just golden and crispy.

Turn the heat down to low, cover, and cook for 10 to 20 minutes, depending on the size of

continued »

the pieces, and check to make sure they're not cooking too fast or at too high a temperature (over 350 degrees F). Remove the lid and turn the chicken again, turning up the heat enough to crisp up the chicken, but being careful that the oil doesn't get too hot. Keep an eye on it and give it a final turn to crisp the other side. Remove from the skillet and keep warm on a baking sheet with a roasting rack. Let the chicken rest for a while so the juices return into the meat. Serve with your favorite sides.

Note: At the restaurant, we use boneless chicken breasts and serve it with mashed potatoes, Magnolias' Collard Greens (page 181), Creamed Corn (page 190), cracked pepper biscuits, and sausage herb gravy.

Oven-Roasted Chicken with Roasted Carrots, Yukon Gold Potatoes, and Lady Peas

SERVES 4

We enjoy roasted chicken at least once a week at my house. It's just easy! This recipe takes about an hour and a half. It's a great dinner for school nights, and the leftovers can be used for a quick chicken salad lunch.

1 large roasting chicken
Kosher salt
Freshly cracked black pepper
1 bunch fresh thyme, split in half
1 garlic head, halved
1 lemon, halved
1/4 stick butter, melted
1 large onion, cut into thick slices
4 carrots, cut into 1 1/2-inch pieces

1 fennel bulb, top removed
  and cut into wedges
1/4 cup olive oil, divided
10 small Yukon Gold potatoes
Lady Peas (recipe follows)

SPECIAL EQUIPMENT
Butcher's twine

Preheat the oven to 350 degrees F.

Remove the giblets from the chicken and rinse the cavity and the outside of the chicken. Sprinkle the inside cavity with salt and pepper. Stuff in a half bunch of thyme, the garlic, and the lemon halves. Brush the outside of the chicken with melted butter and sprinkle with more cracked pepper and salt. Tie the legs together with butcher's twine and tuck the wings back under the body.

In a large roasting pan, combine the onion, carrots, and fennel. Toss the vegetables with 1/8 cup of olive oil, salt, pepper, and the remaining half bunch of thyme. Spread the vegetables around the pan and place the chicken on top.

Roast the chicken in the oven for 50 minutes. Remove from the oven, lightly toss the potatoes with the remaining 1/8 cup of olive oil, and scatter the potatoes around the pan. Return to the oven for an additional 30 to 40 minutes, or until the juices from the chicken run clear. Place the chicken on a cutting board to rest. Spoon the vegetables onto a serving platter. Keep warm until ready to serve. Serve with a side of Lady Peas.

Lady Peas

3 cups fresh lady peas
2 ½ cups water
Smoked pork neck bone or piece
    of smoked bacon (optional)

¾ teaspoon salt
Dash white pepper
2 tablespoons butter

Rinse the peas under cold water and remove any foreign particles. Put them in a saucepan and add the water. Add the smoked product, if desired. Cook over medium heat for 30 to 35 minutes, removing the foam that will appear as the peas begin to cook and discarding it. Season with the salt, white pepper, and butter.

Magnolias' Veal Meatloaf with Butter-Whipped Potatoes, Mushroom and Sage Gravy, and Tobacco Onions

SERVES 6 TO 8

This recipe raises regular old meatloaf to new heights. At the restaurant, we have lunch customers on a call list for when the meatloaf is just coming out of the oven. It's that good!

2 tablespoons light olive oil
2 cups minced yellow onions
2 tablespoons minced garlic
1 1/2 tablespoons minced fresh sage
1 1/2 tablespoons minced fresh oregano
2 tablespoons minced fresh parsley
2 pounds finely ground veal, very well chilled
1 1/4 pounds ground pork or bacon, very well chilled

2 eggs, lightly beaten and chilled
4 tablespoons heavy (whipping) cream
1 tablespoon salt
1 teaspoon freshly ground black pepper
Butter–Whipped Potatoes (recipe follows)
Mushroom and Sage Gravy (page 160)
Tobacco Onions (page 160)
Fresh sage sprigs, for garnishing

In a small heavy-bottom saucepan over medium heat, heat the olive oil. Add the onions and cook until translucent. Add the garlic, sage, oregano, and parsley and cook for 2 minutes, continuing to stir. Remove from the heat and spread out the mixture on a plate or pan. Cool to room temperature and refrigerate to cool completely.

In a mixing bowl, mix together the chilled veal and pork just enough to combine. Add the chilled onion/herb mixture, eggs, cream, salt, and pepper. Mix together until well combined. Put the mixture in the refrigerator to chill.

Prepare the potatoes, gravy, and onions; keep warm.

Preheat the oven to 375 degrees F.

On a baking sheet with raised sides, form the meatloaf mixture into two loaves about 4 inches wide, 1 1/2 inches tall, and 10 inches long; you can also use standard loaf pans. Bake for 45 to 50 minutes, or until the loaves reach an internal temperature of 170 degrees F. Remove from the oven and allow to rest for 5 minutes before slicing and serving. (I like to finish the meatloaf on a hot grill for added flavor and texture.)

Place 1/2 cup of the potatoes in the center of each plate and place two pieces of meatloaf next to the potatoes. Spoon the gravy over the meatloaf and potatoes and garnish with the onions and a sprig of sage.

Butter-Whipped Potatoes

6 cups large roughly cut peeled
    russet or boiling potatoes
6 cups cold water
2 tablespoons plus 1 teaspoon
    fine sea salt, divided

1 cup heavy (whipping) cream
1/2 cup half-and-half
6 tablespoons butter
White pepper

In a saucepan over medium-high heat, bring the potatoes, water, and 2 tablespoons of salt to a boil. Lower the heat to a simmer and cook for 18 to 20 minutes, or until the potatoes are tender when pierced with a fork.

In a small saucepan, heat the cream,

continued »

half-and-half, and butter until the butter has melted. Drain the liquid off the potatoes and return the pan to the burner. Carefully blend the warm cream mixture into the potatoes and whip the potatoes using a hand mixer. Season with the remaining 1 teaspoon of salt and white pepper to taste. Keep warm until ready to serve.

Mushroom and Sage Gravy

MAKES 3 CUPS

3 tablespoons butter
3 tablespoons minced yellow onion
2 cups sliced and roughly chopped assorted mushrooms (such as shiitake, cremini, portobello, morel, and chanterelle)
1 teaspoon minced garlic

2 teaspoons chopped fresh sage
1/4 cup all-purpose flour
2 1/2 cups Chicken Broth (page 19), divided
Salt
Freshly ground black pepper

In a medium saucepan over medium-high heat, melt the butter. Add the onion, mushrooms, garlic, and sage. Cook for 3 to 4 minutes, or until the mushrooms are tender and most of their juices have cooked off. Add the flour and stir until combined. Add half the chicken broth and whisk vigorously until the mixture thickens. Add the remaining 1 1/4 cups of broth and bring back up to a boil. Skim off any foam that may appear and discard. Cook the gravy for 8 to 10 minutes, or until the gravy is smooth and the starchy flavor of the roux is cooked out. Season to taste with salt and pepper. Keep warm until ready to serve.

Tobacco Onions

MAKES 2 CUPS

This dish came by its name because the onions look like tobacco once cooked.

4 cups vegetable oil
1/2 cup all-purpose flour
1 teaspoon salt

1/2 teaspoon freshly ground black pepper
2 cups rings of yellow onions, cut into 1/16-inch-thick slices

In a heavy saucepan with deep sides over medium-high heat, preheat the oil to 340 degrees F. In a small mixing bowl, combine the flour, salt, and pepper. Mix well. Add the onions and evenly coat. Place the onions in the heated oil and stir gently with a skimmer so that they cook evenly. As they begin to become golden brown and caramelized, lift them out of the oil, shake off the excess, and place them on paper towels to cool. The onions will continue to cook for a moment.

Chicken and Andouille Sausage Gumbo

SERVES 12

When I think about good gumbo, I always think about New Orleans. The famous chef Paul Prudhomme started the movement to serve traditional French Creole cuisine in an upscale restaurant. He was followed by Emeril Lagasse and a host of other New Orleans chefs. This is a hearty recipe with all of the delicious things that make gumbo special. Filé powder is a traditional Creole seasoning that can be found in the spice section of most grocery stores.

1 pound boneless, skinless chicken thighs
6 tablespoons peanut oil or canola oil
1/2 cup all–purpose flour
3/4 cup diced celery
1 cup diced onion
1/2 cup diced red bell pepper
1/2 cup diced green bell pepper
1 pound andouille sausage, diced
1/4 cup tomato paste
1 tablespoon minced garlic
1 tablespoon minced fresh thyme
1/2 tablespoon filé powder, plus
  more for sprinkling

1/2 teaspoon red pepper flakes
1 bay leaf
5 cups Chicken Broth (page
  19), room temperature
1 tablespoon fine sea salt
1 1/2 teaspoons freshly ground black pepper
Pinch cayenne pepper
1 1/2 cups sliced fresh okra,
  cut in 1/2–inch slices
2 tablespoons chopped fresh parsley
Carolina Jasmine Rice (page 140)
1/4 cup sliced scallions, for garnishing

Preheat the oven to 375 degrees F.

Place the chicken thighs on a baking sheet with raised sides and roast for 30 to 40 minutes. Remove from the oven and cool. Dice and reserve.

In a heavy-bottom pot over medium-high heat, heat the oil until it just begins to smoke. Carefully add the flour all at once and stir with a wooden spoon. Carefully continue to stir the roux for the next 8 to 10 minutes. During this time, move the entire pan on and off the heat to control a slow, even toasting of the flour; a light mahogany color is optimal. If the flour burns, you will need to discard it and start

over. This roux becomes extremely hot, so be very careful.

When the desired color is obtained, lower the heat to medium and remove the pot from the burner. Carefully add the celery, onion, and red and green bell peppers all at once. This will stop the roux from continuing to brown. Mix the vegetables and roux for 2 minutes, allowing the steam that is produced to be released.

Place the pot back over medium heat and add the sausage, tomato paste, garlic, thyme, filé powder, red pepper flakes, and bay leaf. Stir over medium heat for 2 to 3 minutes, or until the vegetables become soft. Add the

continued »

chicken broth and whisk vigorously. Gradually bring to a boil, then skim off and discard the foam. Continue to cook the gumbo slowly for 7 minutes while stirring occasionally. Add the diced chicken, salt, black pepper, and cayenne pepper. Continue to cook the gumbo over low heat for another 6 minutes. During this process the oil will rise to the top; skim off the oil and discard. Add the okra and parsley and allow the okra to cook gently in the gumbo for 10 to 15 minutes, or until it stops floating. Too much movement will break up the okra. Discard the bay leaf.

Serve by ladling 1 cup of gumbo in each bowl and scooping $1/4$ cup of the rice in the center. Garnish with the scallions and sprinkle with additional filé powder.

Southern Carpetbagger with Roasted Mushroom and Potato Hash, Cornmeal Fried Oysters, Madeira Sauce, and Smoked Blue Cheese Béarnaise

SERVES 4

The decadent Southern Carpetbagger comes on and off Magnolias' menu depending on when local oysters are in season. The dish originated in the United Kingdom in the early 1900s. In early versions, the oyster is stuffed into the filet and sliced, resembling the design of a "carpet bag"—a simplistic purse carried by travelers. For this recipe, we serve our oysters on the side with the other fixings. The presentation is still striking!

4 (12-ounce) New York strip steaks
2 tablespoons olive oil
2 tablespoons Steak Seasoning
 (optional, recipe follows)
Salt
Freshly ground black pepper

Roasted Mushroom and Potato
 Hash (page 166)
Madeira Sauce (page 23)
Cornmeal Fried Oysters (page 51)
Smoked Blue Cheese Béarnaise (page 166)

Preheat the oven to 400 degrees F. Rub the steaks with the olive oil and sprinkle with the steak seasoning, if desired, or just salt and pepper.

In a large cast-iron skillet over high heat, sear the steaks on both sides, about 4 minutes per side. Place the pan in the oven and cook 2 minutes for medium rare, 4 minutes for medium, and 6 to 7 minutes for well done.

Remove the pan from the oven and transfer the steaks to a warm plate to rest. Place 4 plates on the counter. Equally divide the roasted mushroom and potato hash among them. Place the steak on the hash and ladle the Madeira sauce over the steak. Sprinkle the oysters around the perimeter of the plate and finish with a ladle of béarnaise.

Steak Seasoning

MAKES ABOUT ½ CUP

2 tablespoons kosher salt
2 tablespoons freshly cracked black pepper
2 tablespoons smoked paprika
1 tablespoon granulated garlic

1 tablespoon granulated onion
1 tablespoon ground coriander seed
1 tablespoon red pepper flakes

Mix all the ingredients together. Store in an airtight container.

continued »

Roasted Mushroom and Potato Hash

SERVES 4

3 quarts water
1 sweet potato, peeled and
    cut into 1/2-inch dice
1 pound Yukon Gold potatoes,
    peeled and diced
1/2 cup chopped red onion
1/4 cup chopped fresh sage

1 pound assorted mushrooms (such as
    baby portobello, oyster, shiitake, or
    morel), diced into 1/2-inch pieces
1/2 cup olive oil
1/2 cup chopped and cooked bacon
2 cloves minced garlic
2 tablespoons butter
Coarse sea salt
Freshly ground black pepper

Put a baking sheet in the oven and preheat to 400 degrees F. In a medium pot, bring the water to a boil. Add the diced potatoes, turn off the heat, and let sit for 5 minutes, then drain the potatoes. In a large bowl, combine the cooked potatoes, onion, sage, mushrooms, olive oil, bacon, garlic, and butter; season with salt and pepper to taste. Remove the baking sheet from the oven, spread the mixture on the tray, and roast for 15 minutes, occasionally turning the mixture on the tray as it roasts. Remove from the heat and keep warm until ready to serve.

Smoked Blue Cheese Béarnaise

MAKES 1 1/2 CUPS

Use a good smoked blue cheese or substitute smoked Gouda.

1 cup unsalted butter
1/4 cup finely chopped shallots
2 tablespoons chopped tarragon
1/4 cup tarragon vinegar
1/4 cup white wine
1 bay leaf

1/2 teaspoon black peppercorns
3 egg yolks
1/4 cup crumbled smoked blue cheese
Coarse sea salt
Freshly cracked black pepper

To clarify the butter, melt it in a small pot over low heat and do not stir (stirring causes the solids to separate). Remove from the heat and skim the solids floating on top. Keep warm.

In a medium saucepan over medium heat, combine the shallots, tarragon, vinegar, wine, bay leaf, and peppercorns and boil for 5 minutes. You should end up with about

3 tablespoons of the reduction. Strain through a strainer and set off to the side.

Using the double-boiler method, place a pot of water on the stove, and allow to bubble at a high simmer. In a Pyrex or stainless-steel bowl, mix the egg yolks and vinegar reduction and place over the hot water bath, then slowly stream in a third of the clarified butter, whipping constantly. If it starts to get too hot and the eggs start curdling, briefly remove the bowl from the hot water, then return to the heat and slowly whisk in the remaining butter. Remove from the water, add the cheese, and season with salt and pepper to taste. (If using a blender, pour the egg yolks and vinegar in and blend. With the blender running, slowly stream in the clarified butter. Once it emulsifies, turn the blender on high and add remaining butter and cheese and check for seasoning.) Keep warm until ready to serve.

Christmas Prime Rib

SERVES 6 TO 8

This recipe makes a show-stopping main course for the special Christmas dinner. Leftovers can be used for the Roasted Prime Rib Sandwich (page 106).

3–rib roast, from the loin end, 7 to 8 pounds
1 to 2 tablespoons vegetable oil
Salt
Freshly cracked black pepper

Rosemary (optional)
Thyme (optional)
Minced fresh garlic (optional)

Here are four tips to a great prime rib:

BUY A GOOD QUALITY CUT. When you buy a rib roast, there are usually three different options: bone off, 3-bone rib roast, and the larger 6-bone rib roast. When the butcher is cutting the rib roast, they will cut from the 6 rib to the 12 rib. Most butchers will cut that into two sections, 6 to 9 and 10 to 12. Tell them you want the cut closest to the loin; it's less fatty and a little smaller. The ribs get bigger as you move closer to the shoulder. Sometimes the butcher shop will refer to that cut as the "first cut," "loin end," or the "small end." So when placing your order, ask for the first 3 ribs from the loin end, 10 to 12. Let it sit on the counter at room temperature for 3 hours before cooking.

BROWN IT FIRST. Cooking a roast at a lower temperature ensures a much juicier roast than at a high temperature. There is much less moisture loss at a lower temperature. You still want that caramelized exterior on your roast, so brown it first.

To get started, you will need salt and pepper; the amount will depend on you. Vegetable oil, maybe about a tablespoon or two. Have the roast trimmed and tied with butcher twine at both ends. If you have never done this before, ask your butcher to do it for you. It's just to keep its shape when cooking. Pour the oil in the roasting pan and place it over the first two front burners over medium-high heat. Pat dry the prime rib and place it in the pan, cooking on all sides until nicely browned, 7 to 9 minutes. There will be about $1/2$ cup of rendered fat in the bottom of the pan. Remove the roast from the pan and discard the fat from the pan.

ELEVATE IT. Preheat the oven to 200 degrees F. Set a wire rack into the roasting pan. Next, set the roast on the rack and season well with salt, pepper, and additional herbs and garlic if desired. Place the roast on the bottom rack of the oven and cook until a meat thermometer reads 125 degrees F; that will be medium-rare. It will cook for about $3 1/2$ hours. A general rule of thumb when cooking larger cuts of meat is about 30 minutes per pound.

LET IT REST. Remove the roast from the oven and tent with aluminum foil. Let it rest for 20 minutes, then transfer to a carving board to cut and serve.

Precooked Holiday Ham

SERVES 10 TO 12

When buying a ham at the grocery store, it's usually ready to eat. All you are trying to do when cooking is warm it back up and minimize the time in the oven. More time equals a tougher and drier ham. A couple of tricks I've learned from experience: Start with a low oven temperature, around 250 degrees F; choose the right ham; use a hot water bath; and use an oven bag. My best advice is to let the ham rest for about 15 minutes before carving.

1 (8- to 10-pound) spiral-cut bone-in ham
Ham Glaze (recipe follows)

SPECIAL EQUIPMENT
1 large oven bag

The ham will have a plastic or foil covering; leave the cover on the ham. If you suspect there might be a hole in the covering, just wrap the ham tightly with plastic wrap. Rest the ham in a hot water bath for about 90 minutes. (If you don't want to do the water bath method, increase the cooking time to about 15 minutes per pound.)

Remove the ham from the water bath and preheat the oven to 250 degrees F. Unwrap the ham and place on a cutting board or countertop. Some hams will have a plastic disk covering the bone. If yours does, throw it away. Place the ham in the oven roasting bag, pulling tightly for a snug fit. Tie the bag and trim off any excess. Place the ham in a roasting pan, then cut 3 small slits in the top of the bag to prevent it from bursting.

Roast the ham for 70 to 90 minutes, until it reaches an internal temperature of 100 degrees F to 105 degrees F. When the ham reaches the proper temperature, remove the pan from the oven and increase the temperature to 350 degrees F. Carefully cut open the bag and roll it down to expose the ham. Brush all sides with a third of the ham glaze, saving the rest for later. Return the ham to the oven to cook for another 10 minutes. Remove the ham from the oven, brushing with another third of the glaze and allowing it to rest for 15 minutes. Take $1/2$ cup of the pan drippings and pour into a small saucepan over medium-low heat. Stir in the remaining third of the ham glaze to make it into a sauce to serve with the ham.

Ham Glaze

MAKES 1 PINT

My wife, Martha, always serves our holiday ham with this special glaze. It's her father's recipe, and he was from the great state of Alabama. The recipe is written on an old card that gets harder to read every year due to the use. The original glaze called for maraschino cherries, but we now use cherry preserves. You can also use your favorite kind of preserves, too! Feel free to pinch more cloves if desired; it will add a little more spice.

$1/2$ cup white vinegar
$1/4$ cup light corn syrup
6 tablespoons water
2 (12-ounce) jars of cherry
   preserves, or preferred kind

$1/2$ teaspoon cloves
$1/2$ teaspoon nutmeg
$1/2$ teaspoon cinnamon

In a small bowl, whisk together the vinegar, corn syrup, water, preserves, cloves, nutmeg, and cinnamon. Mix well, then pour into a small saucepan over medium heat and bring to a simmer for 4 to 5 minutes. Set aside until ready to use.

Fresh Ham from Scratch

SERVES 12 TO 14

If you want to make your own fresh ham, it takes about nine days to brine and another half day to cook. In Magnolias' kitchen, we used to brine the fresh hams in large bins for about thirty days. A guest chef from Chicago for a Charleston Wine + Food event showed me the trick used here. I thought it was a great idea and it saved precious cooler space! The ham will keep for a month, wrapped and hung up.

1 tablespoon red pepper flakes
2 tablespoons whole cloves
2 tablespoons allspice berries
1 tablespoon whole coriander
5 bay leaves
2 star anise pods
¾ cup granulated sugar
¾ cup kosher salt

2 tablespoons pink curing salt
3 cups cold water
1 (25–pound) fresh ham, give
   or take a few pounds

SPECIAL EQUIPMENT
Butcher injecting needle

You must keep the ham cold at all times during the brining process!

In a 2-quart saucepan, combine all the spices, sugar, and salts. Add the water and bring to a boil over medium heat, stirring until salt and sugar dissolve. Remove the pot from the stove and allow the brine to cool overnight in the refrigerator.

Place the ham in a container big enough to hold it and small enough that it fits in the refrigerator or a cooler.

Turn the ham so you can see the vein that runs by the bone. It's in the open end of the leg toward the direction of the knee cap. Give it a squeeze. A little blood will come out. Not much, but enough to know where it is. Strain the brine, making sure to keep it really cold. Fill the injection needle with the brining solution and slowly inject the solution into the vein, taking breaks between injections so the ham has time to absorb the liquid. Repeat the process until you have injected all of the brine. Wrap the ham tightly with plastic wrap and refrigerate for 9 days.

Heat the smoker to 225 degrees F. We use a wood mixture of oak, apple, or peach, and just a little pecan to smoke our hams and bacon. Cook the ham for about 6 hours at 225 degrees F, then increase the heat to 325 degrees F and cook until the ham registers 155 degrees F internally on the meat thermometer. Check frequently. Make sure to check the temperature in the joints and bone. Depending on the smoker and ham size, it can take from 8 to 12 hours total cooking time.

Thanksgiving Turkey

SERVES 10 TO 12

To say that Thanksgiving is a busy day at Magnolias is an understatement. We serve America's traditional holiday meal to approximately nine hundred people each year! In order to feed these masses, we brine sixty-five turkeys overnight and cook them the next day. To keep the birds moist, I rub sage butter under the skin and baste the turkeys with melted butter every 25 minutes or so. I separate the legs from the breast and cook them at different temperatures and times. The breast is cooked at 200 degrees F and the legs at 325 degrees F with internal temperatures reaching 165 degrees F and 195 degrees F, respectively.

2 cups brown sugar

2 cups coarse sea salt

1 bunch fresh thyme

3 bay leaves

2 tablespoons black peppercorns

1 (18– to 20–pound) turkey, giblets
  and neck removed

Sage Butter (page 174)

Stuffing (page 174)

2 carrots, peeled and chopped

1 yellow onion, chopped

2 celery ribs, chopped

6 garlic cloves, smashed

Giblet Gravy (page 175)

For the turkey brine, bring 1 1/2 gallons of water to a boil in a stockpot and add the brown sugar, salt, thyme, bay leaves, and peppercorns. Stir until the sugar and salt dissolve. Remove from the heat and add 1 gallon of cold water or ice. Allow the brine to come to room temperature. Submerge the turkey in the brine and let sit overnight in the refrigerator or a cool place for 12 to 24 hours. Remove the turkey from brine, rinse well, and pat dry.

Prepare the sage butter and stuffing.

Preheat the oven to 325 degrees F. Scatter the carrots, onion, celery, and garlic in the bottom of a heavy-duty roasting pan and add 3 cups of water. Set a roasting rack in the pan. Take a good handful of the sage butter and rub it under the turkey skin and all over the outside of the bird. Spoon the stuffing into the cavity and tie the legs together with kitchen twine. (If the bird is already trussed, skip this step.) Set the turkey on the rack with the vegetables and roast in the oven, basting with the pan drippings every 25 minutes until the thigh juice runs clear and the internal temperature of the stuffing reaches 165 degrees F, about 3 1/2 hours. Transfer the turkey to a carving board and cover loosely with foil. Let the bird rest about 20 minutes before carving. Serve with giblet gravy.

continued »

Sage Butter

MAKES 2 CUPS

1 pound unsalted butter, cubed
1 1/2 cups turkey fat or duck fat
1 bunch fresh sage, chopped

3 garlic cloves, crushed and minced
1 tablespoon coarse sea salt
2 teaspoons white pepper

In the bowl of a stand mixer, whip the butter with a paddle attachment until soft, about 3 minutes. Slowly add the fat, sage, garlic, salt, and white pepper, mixing well. Transfer to an airtight container and refrigerate. The butter can be prepared ahead of time and stored in the refrigerator for up to 1 week.

Stuffing

MAKES 1 QUART

6 tablespoons butter
1 pound Italian sausage, casing removed
2 large yellow onions, diced
2 ribs celery, diced
2 garlic cloves, minced
4 cups Chicken Broth (page 19), divided, plus more if needed

1 large bag stuffing, or 10 cups cubed day–old bread
1 teaspoon fresh thyme
1 tablespoon poultry seasoning
1 teaspoon coarse sea salt
Freshly ground black pepper
1 cup dried cranberries
1 cup diced Granny Smith apples

In a large, heavy-bottom pan, melt the butter, then sauté the sausage, breaking it up with a wooden spoon. Cook until most of the pink is gone, then add the onions, celery, and garlic and cook until soft. Pour in 3 cups of the chicken stock and bring to a boil, then add the bread. Cook until well mixed and the bread is soft, adding more chicken stock if needed. Add the thyme, poultry seasoning, salt, pepper to taste, cranberries, and apples. Check for seasoning and remove from heat. The stuffing can be made a day ahead of time and stored in the refrigerator, but bring it to room temperature before stuffing the bird.

Giblet Gravy

1 onion, chopped
1 celery rib, chopped
Giblets from the turkey (heart,
    neck, gizzards, and liver)

Pan drippings from roasted
    turkey or unsalted butter
1/2 cup all–purpose flour
Salt
Freshly ground black pepper

In a large pot of cold water (about 6 cups), bring the onion, celery, and giblets to a boil. Reduce to a simmer and cook uncovered for 90 minutes. Strain the stock through a fine-mesh sieve, reserving the stock and giblets and set aside.

Tilt the roasting pan to remove the vegetables and skim off the fat, measuring out 1/2 cup of drippings. Use the drippings and flour to make a roux in a small saucepan over low heat, cooking about 5 minutes to a light, nutty color and flavor, and remove from the heat.

Place the roasting pan across two burners over medium heat and stir the reserved stock into the drippings, scraping up all the brown bits. Slowly add the roux to the pan, whisking constantly to prevent lumps. Reduce the heat and simmer to desired thickness. Pass the gravy through a strainer, add the chopped giblets, and season with salt and pepper to taste.

SIDES

Dirty Rice

Is it Creole? Cajun? Is it a French dish that someone got hold of down in New Orleans and changed up with Southern ingredients? Who knows! Whatever the origin, it's really good! The rice has a lot of different uses: as a stuffing for game birds of all kinds, a side dish for fish, and even as a main course for a casual supper.

6 ounces spicy Italian sausage
1/4 pound raw chicken livers
3 tablespoons plus 1 teaspoon
  olive oil, divided
Salt
Freshly ground black pepper
1/2 cup finely chopped yellow onions

1 tablespoon minced garlic
1/4 cup chopped tasso ham
2 cups parboiled rice
2 3/4 cups Chicken Broth (page 19)
1/2 cup chopped green onions
Tabasco

Preheat the oven to 400 degrees F.

Place the Italian sausage on a baking sheet with raised sides. Use the top rack of the oven and bake for 10 to 15 minutes or until the sausage is firm and its juices run clear. Allow to cool and cut into small bite-size pieces. Reduce the oven heat to 350 degrees F.

In a glass or stainless-steel bowl, toss the livers, 1 teaspoon of the olive oil, and a dash of salt and pepper. Transfer the livers to a baking sheet and place it on the top rack of the oven. Bake for 20 minutes. Cool the livers, finely chop them, and set aside.

In a heavy-bottom oven-safe saucepan, heat the remaining 3 tablespoons of olive oil over medium heat. Add the onions and garlic and sauté, stirring, for 2 to 3 minutes, or until the onions are translucent. Add the sausage, tasso, and chicken livers and sauté for 3 minutes. Add the rice and stir until it is coated by the olive oil.

Pour in the chicken broth and bring the mixture to a boil, constantly stirring. Cover the saucepan and place it in the oven. Bake for 20 to 30 minutes or until all of the liquid is absorbed and the rice is tender. Uncover the saucepan, add the green onions, and fluff the rice and onions with a fork. Season with salt, black pepper, and Tabasco to taste. Serve immediately.

Red Rice

This recipe is Magnolias' chef Ms. Marshall's interpretation of the Lowcountry's famous red rice. The original version—jollof rice—came to the United States from the West African coast sometime in the mid-1700s. When at home, one way I like to prepare red rice is in a Dutch oven. Smithey is a local Charleston company that makes some of the best cast-iron cookware I've found, and their Dutch oven is fantastic. Their information is in the Resources section of this book (page 216).

Red rice is a menu staple at the restaurant and has been enjoyed over the years by many repeat customers, including professional athletes, Hollywood celebrities, and one of our favorite U.S. senators.

1/4 cup vegetable oil or canola oil
8 ounces diced smoked sausage
6 ounces diced tasso ham
4 pieces diced applewood-smoked bacon
1 large onion, finely diced
1 bell pepper of choice, finely diced
2 celery ribs, finely diced
1 (6-ounce) can tomato paste

2 cups tomato juice
1 cup water
1 chicken bouillon cube
3 tablespoons sugar
1/2 teaspoon granulated garlic
1/2 teaspoon granulated onion
1/2 teaspoon cayenne pepper
2 cups uncooked Uncle Ben's or parboiled rice

Preheat the oven to 350 degrees F.

In a large frying pan or Dutch oven, heat the oil over medium-high heat. Add the sausage, tasso, and bacon. Cook until the bacon has rendered, about 5 minutes. Add the onion, bell pepper, and celery and cook until the vegetables have softened, 3 to 4 minutes. Stir in the tomato paste, tomato juice, water, and bouillon cube. Mix well, then add the sugar, granulated garlic, granulated onion, and cayenne pepper. Stir again. Bring to a light boil and remove from heat.

If using a frying pan, transfer contents to a Dutch oven or 9 x 13-inch baking dish. Pour in the rice and stir well. Place a tightly fitted lid on top of the Dutch oven, or wrap the baking dish with plastic wrap, then foil, and bake for 45 minutes. Turn off the oven and allow the rice to rest in the oven for an additional 10 minutes. Remove the rice from the oven, stir, and serve.

Magnolias' Collard Greens

Magnolias makes the best collard greens! There are many varieties of these hearty Southern greens and they're typically at their best after the first big frost and in the months from November to April. A few fun facts: In June of 2011, former UN Ambassador Nikki Haley, then governor of South Carolina, signed a bill naming collard greens the state vegetable. It's a Southern New Year's Day tradition to eat these greens to ensure a prosperous year ahead.

2 large or 3 small bunches collard greens
2 tablespoons olive oil
1 cup diced yellow onion, cut into ¼-inch dice
1 tablespoon minced garlic
1 smoked ham hock or 2 smoked
   pork neck bones

3 tablespoons apple cider vinegar
9 cups Chicken Broth (page 19)
2 teaspoons Tabasco, divided
Salt
Freshly ground black pepper

Wash the collard greens very thoroughly with cold water, remove the center stem, and the large ribs, and give them a rough chop. They should be leafy, and you need about 12 cups. In a large heavy-bottom stockpot over medium heat, heat the olive oil. Add the onion and garlic and sauté for 2 to 3 minutes, stirring, or until the onions are translucent. Add the ham hock and vinegar and gradually add the collard greens. Cook the greens over medium heat, stirring occasionally, until they are all wilted. As they wilt you will have enough room to get them all into the pot. Add the chicken broth and 1 teaspoon of Tabasco. Bring to a boil and simmer for 1 hour and 45 minutes to 2 hours, adding more chicken broth if needed, 1 cup at a time, until the greens have a good flavor and are silky in texture.

Add the remaining 1 teaspoon of Tabasco, if desired, and salt and pepper to taste.

Three Greens

This is a dish I created for the 1994 Magnolias James Beard House dinner in New York City. It was a great surprise: The three different flavors and textures of the greens made a real winner. I've been honored to cook at the Beard House many times during my career. New York is so fast-paced that the details of the events run together, but they're always an adventure and always lots of fun!

1 tablespoon olive oil

1 cup diced yellow onions, cut into ½-inch dice

2 teaspoons minced garlic

3 tablespoons apple cider vinegar

6 cups Chicken Broth (page 19), divided

6 cups washed, stemmed, and roughly chopped collard greens

6 cups washed, stemmed, and roughly chopped mustard greens

4 cups washed, stemmed, and roughly chopped watercress

¼ teaspoon freshly ground black pepper

Salt

Tabasco

In a large, heavy-bottom stockpot over medium heat, heat the oil. Add the onions and garlic and sauté for 2 to 3 minutes, stirring, or until the onions are translucent. Add the vinegar and 3 cups of the chicken broth and bring to a boil. Add the collards and simmer for 30 minutes, stirring occasionally. Add the remaining 3 cups of chicken broth and the mustard greens and simmer for 15 minutes. Add the watercress and simmer for 15 minutes. Finish with the black pepper and season to taste with salt and Tabasco.

Butter Beans

I could live on beans and rice! Southern butter beans come in various varieties, such as speckled and lima (pronounced "LIME-ah"). Some Southern cooks prefer to cook their beans with smoked turkey necks, pork tails, or ham hocks for added flavor. They will simmer them in the pot for a couple of hours until they are creamy and soft—like butter.

2 tablespoons butter
$\frac{1}{2}$ cup diced onion, cut into $\frac{1}{4}$-inch dice
1 teaspoon minced garlic
4 cups fresh butter beans (1 $\frac{1}{2}$ to 2 pounds)

6 cups Chicken Broth (page 19)
$\frac{1}{4}$ teaspoon freshly ground black pepper
1 smoked pork neck bone or
    ham hock (optional)

In a large, heavy-bottom saucepan over medium heat, melt the butter. Add the onion and garlic and sauté, stirring constantly, for 2 to 3 minutes, or until the onions are translucent. Add the butter beans and chicken broth. Season with ground pepper and add the neck bone (if using). Bring to a simmer over medium heat, skimming off the foam as it appears.

For a side dish of butter beans, allow them to cook uncovered for a total time of 50 to 55 minutes. If cooking them for succotash (page 184), reduce the cooking time to 20 minutes, or until the beans are tender but still whole.

Remove the neck bone. The broth will have reduced to 1 cup or so. Reduce the heat and break up some of the beans with a whisk or spoon until the remainder of the broth is thickened by the starch of the beans. Remove from heat and let cool.

If you have to use frozen beans, reduce the cooking time. The cooking procedure will be the same, but use 2 cups less of broth and reduce the cooking time by 25 minutes.

Succotash

SERVES 4

Succotash is a dish that was introduced as a stew to the American colonists in the seventeenth century. Succotash recipes migrated South and now appear in countless forms. This recipe came from Magnolias' chef Casey Taylor's Tennessee roots. The combination of shrimp and vegetables makes an excellent accompaniment to grilled fish or chicken. The chicken gravy gives it depth and helps to bring the flavors together.

1 teaspoon olive oil
1/2 cup diced red onion, cut into 1/2-inch dice
1 teaspoon minced garlic
1/2 cup diced red peppers, cut into 1/2-inch dice
1 1/2 cups Cooked Yellow Corn Kernels (recipe follows)
2 cups cooked fresh Butter Beans (page 183) or preferred summer bean

20 large shrimp, peeled and deveined
2 cups washed, stemmed, and julienned spinach, cut in 1/4-inch strips
1 cup Chicken Gravy (page 22)
1/2 cup Chicken Broth (page 19)
Salt
Freshly ground black pepper

In a heavy-bottom saucepan over medium heat, heat the oil. Add the onion, garlic, red peppers, and corn and sauté, stirring, for 2 to 3 minutes, or until the onions become translucent. Add the butter beans and mix well. Add the shrimp, spinach, chicken gravy, and chicken broth. Simmer, stirring, until the shrimp are pink.

Season with salt and pepper to taste. Serve immediately.

Cooked Yellow Corn Kernels

MAKES 2 CUPS

3 cups water
1 teaspoon kosher salt

4 yellow corn ears, shucked

In a heavy-bottom stockpot, bring the water and salt to a boil. Put the fresh corn in the boiling water and cook for 8 minutes. Drain the corn and rinse with cold water.

Fill a large bowl with ice and water. Put drained corn in the ice water to stop the cooking. Drain and pat dry. Cut the kernels off the cob by slicing with a sharp knife. This should yield about 2 cups of corn kernels.

Mustard Slaw

As I've said before, I'm a huge fan of coleslaw. This slaw is particularly delicious on barbecue, hot dogs, and grilled sandwiches, or with fried seafood. Keeping a couple of the cabbage's dark green outer leaves adds color and texture to the dish.

MUSTARD SLAW DRESSING
1 1/2 tablespoons apple cider vinegar
1/2 cup Duke's mayonnaise
1 tablespoon whole-grain mustard
1 teaspoon freshly ground black pepper
1 teaspoon sugar

SLAW
1 medium cabbage (approximately 6 cups)
1 tightly packed cup grated carrot
  (approximately 2 large carrots)

To make the mustard slaw dressing: In a medium bowl, whisk the vinegar into the mayonnaise until smooth. Add the mustard, pepper, and sugar and whisk to incorporate. The dressing will keep well for several days in the refrigerator.

To make the slaw: Remove the cabbage's tougher outer dark green leaves, but reserve 2 or 3 tender ones to use. Wash the cabbage leaves free of all sand and dirt, then julienne the outer leaves. Cut the cabbage in half and remove and discard the white core. Slice thin.

When ready to serve, mix the cabbage, carrots, and dressing. Place in the refrigerator for 10 minutes to allow a slight softening of the cabbage. The slaw will keep in the refrigerator for 24 hours.

Potato Salad

Don't put a bowl of potato salad in front of me and expect to have any left! My mother always made hers the night before so that the flavors came out more. This dish goes well with most meats and, of course, is a great "covered dish" to bring to a party.

5 pounds russet potatoes, washed
2 cups Miracle Whip
1 cup sweet pickle relish
1 tablespoon Dijon mustard
1 tablespoon yellow mustard
1 tablespoon white vinegar
1 tablespoon celery seed

1 tablespoon chopped fresh dill,
    plus more for garnishing
$1/2$ teaspoon paprika, plus more for garnishing
1 teaspoon salt, plus more to taste
5 hard-boiled eggs, peeled and chopped
3 celery ribs, diced
Freshly ground black pepper

Cut the potatoes into quarters and put them in a large pot. Fill the pot with cold water until the potatoes are covered. Cook the potatoes on the stove over high heat until fork tender, 13 to 15 minutes.

While the potatoes are cooking, make the dressing. In a medium bowl, combine the Miracle Whip, relish, mustards, vinegar, celery seed, dill, and paprika; stir until well combined. Add in the salt, eggs, and celery.

Once the potatoes are tender, drain off all the water and remove any loose potato skins that might have come off during cooking. Rough chop the potatoes into $1/2$-inch chunks. Transfer to the bowl of dressing and mix until all the potatoes are well coated. Check for seasoning and add more salt and pepper if needed. Garnish with additional chopped dill and paprika.

Note: I only add salt to the dressing. Some potatoes get mushy and watery if you salt them when boiling.

Ms. Marshall's Mac and Cheese

SERVES 10 TO 12

Marshall Tucker, aka "Ms. Marshall," has been working with me at Magnolias for many years. She makes the best red rice, mac and cheese, and collard greens you've ever tasted! Truth be told, I think she walks around with a bag of secret spices in her pocket. I don't know the names of the secret spices, but whatever they are, the magic never fails in her recipes. This mac and cheese serves a crowd and works well for a Sunday family dinner or as a Thanksgiving side.

1 1/2 gallons water
4 tablespoons sea salt, divided
8 cups elbow macaroni
5 cups heavy (whipping) cream
1 cup sour cream

1/2 cup prepared mustard
1 tablespoon butter
6 eggs, beaten
9 cups shredded yellow cheddar
   cheese, divided

Preheat the oven to 350 degrees F.

In a large stockpot, bring the water to a boil. Add 2 tablespoons of the salt just before adding the macaroni and cook until al dente, about 12 minutes. Remember, the noodles are going to be cooked again, so don't overcook them. Drain and rinse the elbows in cold water with a few ice cubes to quickly cool. Don't oil the noodles. Transfer the macaroni to a large bowl, cover loosely, and set aside.

In another bowl, combine the heavy cream, sour cream, mustard, butter, remaining 2 tablespoons salt, the eggs, and 6 cups of cheddar cheese. Mix well and pour the mixture over the macaroni, making sure it's well coated. Pour into a large baking dish and cover with foil. Bake for 30 minutes. Pull the dish from the oven and remove the foil; sprinkle the remaining 3 cups of cheddar cheese on top. Return to the oven uncovered and allow the cheese to brown just a little, about 15 minutes. Remove from the oven and enjoy immediately.

Creamed Corn

Homemade creamed corn is more elegant than canned, and it's still an easy and quick recipe to prepare. This recipe has turmeric, which adds a nice color. The rosemary sprig is also unique and infuses an interesting flavor. Be sure to use corn cut fresh from the cob. I'm a big fan of Silver Queen corn—I think it's a little sweeter!

8 fresh corn ears, shucked and cleaned of silk
1 tablespoon unsalted butter
1/2 cup finely diced yellow onion
2 pinches kosher salt
1 fresh rosemary sprig
1 1/2 tablespoons sugar (optional)

1/4 teaspoon turmeric
2 tablespoons yellow cornmeal or cornstarch
1 1/2 cups heavy cream or milk
White pepper
1/4 cup freshly grated Parmesan
  cheese (optional)

Cut the kernels from the corn cobs and place in a mixing bowl. Using the back of the knife, scrape the cobs to remove any corn milk and leftover pulp.

In a saucepan over medium heat, combine the butter and onion and sweat the onion until translucent. Add the salt, corn, and pulp mixture and continue to cook over medium heat. The corn will start to release its juices and tighten a little. Add the whole rosemary sprig to the pan and sprinkle with sugar (if using) and turmeric; stir continuously for 4 to 5 minutes. Add the cornmeal and whisk well. Whisk in the heavy cream and cook until the corn has softened, about 5 minutes. Remove the rosemary sprig and season with white pepper to taste. Finish with the Parmesan cheese, if desired.

SOUTHERN SWEETS

Summer Berries with Grand Marnier and Brown Sugar Sabayon

SERVES 4

This classic French dessert sauce is easy to prepare and can be modified with the addition of different citrus or flavored liqueurs. Feel free to use any combination of berries, or just by themselves: blueberries, strawberries, raspberries, or blackberries. Don't forget the ice cream!

6 egg yolks
1/4 cup light brown sugar
2 tablespoons Grand Marnier

1 teaspoon orange zest
2 pints strawberries, blueberries, raspberries
   or blackberries, or a combination

Place a saucepan filled with water over medium-high heat. In a stainless-steel bowl, combine the egg yolks, brown sugar, Grand Marnier, and orange zest; place the bowl on top of the saucepan. Whisk the mixture vigorously using a whisk for 3 to 4 minutes, or until the mixture triples in volume. The temperature should read 140 degrees F on an instant-read thermometer. When cooked enough, the sabayon will have a shiny sheen and leave obvious ribbons when the whisk is lifted out. Remove from the heat and serve immediately over the berries, or place over a bowl of ice water and stir occasionally to cool completely, then pour into a storage container, cover, and refrigerate 1 hour.

Magnolias' Fruit Cobbler

MAKES 1 (9 X 13-INCH) PAN

Warm cobbler topped with vanilla bean ice cream is hard to beat. Any fruit in season works for this recipe, but I must say my favorites are peaches or blackberries—either used alone or mixed together. You can use frozen fruit if that's all that's available, but you may have to decrease the sugar in the filling by 1/2 cup.

FILLING
9 cups fresh fruit
1 1/2 cups sugar
1 tablespoon lemon juice
1/2 cup White Lily all-purpose flour
1/2 teaspoon salt

TOPPING
6 tablespoons cold unsalted butter, diced
1 1/2 cups White Lily all-purpose flour
1/2 cup sugar
1/2 teaspoon Rumford baking powder*
1/2 teaspoon salt
1/4 cup plus 1 tablespoon buttermilk

To make the filling: In a large bowl, combine all the ingredients, tossing the fruit until it is coated by the other ingredients. Pour the fruit into a 9 x 13-inch baking pan.

Preheat the oven to 350 degrees F.

To make the topping: Keep the butter in the refrigerator while you assemble the remaining ingredients for the topping. In a large bowl, combine the flour, sugar, baking powder, and salt and stir to mix well. Add the diced butter and cut it into the flour with either a pastry cutter or 2 forks until the mixture is crumbly. Add the buttermilk a little at a time until the dough starts to come together. However, this dough should not form a ball like pie dough does. The topping should still very crumbly and not sticky. Sprinkle the topping over the filling. It should be about 1/2 inch thick.

Place the cobbler on the middle rack in the oven for 1 hour, or until the topping is a light golden color and the fruit filling is bubbling up around the sides. Remove the cobbler from the oven and allow it to cool for a few minutes. Serve hot; I prefer mine with ice cream and whipped cream.

*Note: The best baking powder to use in this recipe is aluminum-free baking powder, which contains no sodium aluminum sulfate, so it lacks the metallic taste. Rumford is a good brand of aluminum-free baking powder, found in most grocery stores.

Warm Cream Cheese Brownies

MAKES 1 (9 X 13-INCH) PAN

Brownies have been on Magnolias' menu from day one. Our friends Nancy and Norman Smith, aka "Punch and Honey," are the home cooks behind the original recipe. Over time, this recipe has evolved into the one featured here.

Nonstick cooking spray
1 1/2 cups all-purpose flour
1 1/2 cups cocoa powder
1/4 teaspoon salt
7 eggs
3 1/2 cups granulated sugar
2 teaspoons vanilla extract
3 sticks butter, melted

1/4 cup vegetable oil
1 cup toasted pecans
Vanilla Cream Cheese Filling (recipe follows)
Fudge Sauce (page 198)
Caramel Sauce (page 198)
Vanilla or white chocolate ice cream
Whipped Cream (page 200)

Preheat the oven to 350 degrees F and grease a 9 x 13-inch baking pan with a nonstick cooking spray.

In a medium bowl, sift together the flour, cocoa powder, and salt and set aside. In a separate medium bowl using a whip attachment, beat the eggs, gradually adding the sugar, until the eggs are thick and fluffy. Slowly add the vanilla extract, butter, and oil.

On low speed, slowly blend in the flour mixture until combined. Stir in the toasted pecans. Evenly spoon the batter into the prepared baking pan. Put the cream cheese filling into a piping bag and pipe thick lines on top of the batter. Use a skewer or butter knife to pull through the lines of cream cheese filling in a back-and-forth motion. Bake the brownies for 35 to 40 minutes, or until a cake tester comes out clean.

On the base of each plate, make a decorative pattern of fudge and caramel sauces. Place the brownie in the center of the pattern and top with ice cream and whipped cream.

Vanilla Cream Cheese Filling

MAKES 2 CUPS

4 tablespoons all-purpose flour
3/4 cup powdered sugar
8 ounces cream cheese, room temperature

2 eggs
2 teaspoons vanilla extract
Pinch salt

Sift the flour and powdered sugar together into a medium bowl. Beat the cream cheese with the flour/sugar mixture until well blended. Add the eggs one at a time, beating well and scraping the bowl throughout the process. Beat in the vanilla and salt. Set aside the mixture until ready to use.

continued »

Fudge Sauce

1 cup heavy cream
8 ounces semisweet chocolate

1 teaspoon vanilla extract

In a heavy-bottom saucepan over medium heat, bring the cream to a simmer. Remove the saucepan from the stove and add the chocolate. Allow to sit for 1 minute, then whisk continuously until the chocolate has melted and the sauce is smooth. Whisk in the vanilla extract. Pour into a heat-safe storage container until ready to use.

Caramel Sauce

1½ cups granulated sugar
⅓ cup water
3 tablespoons butter

1½ cups heavy cream
Pinch salt

In a heavy-bottom medium saucepan, combine the sugar and water. (This is the only time you need to stir the sugar; otherwise, crystallization can occur. Also, make sure there is no sugar on the inside edges of the pot to prevent crystallization.)

Place the saucepan over medium to low heat until the sugars start to dissolve, 5 to 10 minutes. Turn the heat up to medium-high and cook until the sugar starts to caramelize, 5 to 7 minutes. The mixture will be an amber color, similar to tea. Do not stir while this is happening. Watch the pot closely, because it goes from caramel to burnt quickly. Turn off the heat and stand back to avoid splattering. Slowly add the butter and cream. Don't panic—the cream will bubble violently, and the caramel might solidify. Simmer over low heat, stirring constantly until the caramel dissolves and the sauce is smooth, about 1 minute. Add the salt and allow the sauce to cool to room temperature. It will thicken as it sits. The caramel sauce can be cooled more quickly with an ice bath.

Sweet Biscuits with Strawberries, Whipped Cream, and Orange Custard Sauce

MAKES 8 (2 1/2-INCH) BISCUITS

Allow me to share a funny story with this dessert: Many years ago, I was invited to participate in the Great Chefs of the South *series hosted by Food & Wine. I was getting ready to make sweet biscuits for about three hundred people and* all *of the event's chefs were standing around the mixer talking. I finished pouring ten bags of White Lily flour into the big floor mixer along with some sugar and baking powder. I turned the mixer to 1 and switched it on . . . and flour went everywhere and my fellow chefs and I were covered! Fortunately, they had a good sense of humor and we all started laughing.*

On our mixer at Magnolias, 1 is low speed and 3 straight down is the highest. That kitchen had the same Hobart mixer we have, but an older model. Sometime in the past the dial had been turned backwards so 1 was fast and 3 was slow. Gun-shy now, I always check the speed first *before mixing!*

7 tablespoons cold salted butter

2 cups plus 2 tablespoons White Lily all–purpose flour, plus more for flouring

7 tablespoons sugar, divided

1 tablespoon Rumford baking powder*

3/4 teaspoon salt

1/2 cup buttermilk

2 tablespoons heavy (whipping) cream

Strawberries (page 200)

Whipped Cream (page 200)

Orange Custard Sauce (page 200)

Preheat the oven to 375 degrees F.

Dice the butter, put it on a plate, and place it in the refrigerator to remain cold while assembling the other ingredients. In a medium bowl, combine the flour, 3 tablespoons of sugar, the baking powder, and the salt. Add the diced butter and cut into the flour with either a pastry cutter or 2 forks until the mixture is crumbly.

Add the buttermilk a little at a time until the dough comes together and forms a ball. Place it on a floured surface, sprinkle it with more flour, and pat it out to a 1-inch-thick circle. Cut the biscuits with a 2 1/2-inch biscuit cutter and place them on a heavy baking sheet. Brush the tops of the biscuits with cream and sprinkle generously with the remaining 4 tablespoons of sugar.

Place the baking sheet on the middle shelf of the oven and bake for 15 to 20 minutes. Remove and cool to room temperature.

Split the biscuits and place the bottom half on each plate. Spoon the strawberries over the bottom halves, add a dollop of whipped cream, and replace the tops. Spoon orange custard sauce around the edges.

Note: The best baking powder to use in this recipe is aluminum-free baking powder, which contains no sodium aluminum sulfate, so it lacks the metallic taste. Rumford is a good brand of aluminum-free baking powder, found in most grocery stores.

continued »

Strawberries

2 pints strawberries, washed, stemmed, and sliced

2 tablespoons sugar

When ready to serve the biscuits, toss the sliced strawberries with the sugar and let them sit for 5 minutes before plating them.

The combination of the sugars and the natural juices of the strawberries will produce a nice strawberry syrup.

Whipped Cream

1 cup heavy cream
1 1/2 tablespoons sugar
1/4 teaspoon pure vanilla extract

Pour the cold cream into a chilled mixing bowl. Whip in the sugar slowly, then add the vanilla. Continue to whip until the cream has tripled in volume and is firm yet creamy.

Orange Custard Sauce

2 cups heavy (whipping) cream
1/2 cup sugar, divided
Zest of 1/2 orange

1/4 vanilla bean, split lengthwise, or 1/2 teaspoon pure vanilla extract
5 egg yolks

In a heavy-bottom saucepan over medium heat, heat the cream with half the sugar, the orange zest, and the vanilla bean. In a separate bowl, vigorously beat the egg yolks with the other 1/4 cup of the sugar until combined. Continue to heat the cream over low to medium heat until there are small bubbles around the edges. Slowly stream half the hot cream into the egg yolk mixture, stirring constantly. When half the cream is incorporated into the egg mixture, slowly pour the mixture back into the pan of hot cream, stirring continuously.

Place the pan over low heat, stirring constantly with a wooden spoon. Cook the custard until it is thick enough to coat the back of the spoon; strain into a storage container. Take out the vanilla bean and scrape the seeds from the pod into the custard. Discard the vanilla bean and orange zest. Cool the custard sauce immediately in an ice bath. Cover and refrigerate for up to 3 days. Serve cold.

Coconut Cream Pie with Banana Custard Sauce and Caramelized Bananas

This pie is easy to prepare and the classic combination of coconut and bananas is delicious. The finished pie is a statement-making dessert, and for a more sophisticated look, you can make eight individual tarts in miniature tart pans. Short dough crust is sweeter and more cookie-like than a traditional pie crust. Keep an eye on the bottom of the pie shells—the short dough pie crust can brown pretty quickly.

Short Dough (recipe follows)
Coconut Cream Filling (page 204)
Cream Topping (page 204)

Banana Custard Sauce (page 205)
Caramelized Bananas (page 205)

Prepare the short dough pie shell for either a whole pie or for tartlets. While is it baking, prepare the coconut cream filling. While the filling is chilling, prepare the cream topping. Pour the filling into the pie shell and immediately spread the cream topping over the top of the pie. Refrigerate for 1 hour or until ready to serve.

Prepare the banana custard sauce and refrigerate until ready to serve.

Just prior to serving, prepare the caramelized bananas. Cut the pie into 8 to 10 slices and serve with a small amount of banana custard sauce and 2 or 3 slices of caramelized bananas.

Short Dough

$3/4$ cup sugar
$3/4$ cup butter, softened
4 cups White Lily all-purpose flour

$1 1/2$ teaspoons salt
2 eggs, lightly beaten

In a large mixing bowl, cream the sugar and butter together until light and fluffy, about 5 minutes. Add the flour and salt and mix until just combined. Add the eggs and mix until just combined. Divide the mixture in half and reserve one half to freeze for future use. Roll out the remaining dough on a floured surface until about $3/16$-inch thick and larger around than the pie tin or tart shell. Gently roll the dough onto the rolling pin and press into

continued »

the pie tin. Trim off the edges, leaving enough dough attached to make a nice crimped edge. Refrigerate until firm.

Preheat the oven to 350 degrees F.

When ready to bake, pierce the bottom of the crust a few times with the tip of a knife. Place the pie tin on a baking sheet and bake it for 12 to 15 minutes, or until it is a light golden color, rotating the pan 180 degrees halfway through. If the pastry dough "domes" on the bottom, gently press it down with a kitchen towel when rotating the pan. Remove from the oven and cool to room temperature.

Note: The extra pie dough can be frozen for up to 3 months.

Coconut Cream Filling

MAKES 1 QUART

1 cup sugar
1/2 cup cornstarch
1 1/2 teaspoons powdered gelatin
1/2 teaspoon salt
1/2 cup coconut milk

3 egg yolks, lightly beaten
2 1/2 cups whole milk
1/2 teaspoon almond extract
1 teaspoon pure vanilla extract
1 1/2 cups shredded coconut

In a large bowl, combine the sugar, cornstarch, gelatin, and salt. Whisk thoroughly, then add the coconut milk and egg yolks; stir to combine.

In a heavy-bottom saucepan over medium heat, heat the milk until there are small bubbles around the edges. Slowly pour the hot milk into the egg yolk mixture, whisking constantly. Pour the mixture back into the saucepan. Cook over medium heat, stirring constantly for about 3 minutes or until very thick. Remove from the heat. Stir in the extracts and coconut. Allow the mixture to cool completely in an ice bath, stirring frequently. Use when cooled or transfer to a storage container, cover, and refrigerate overnight.

Cream Topping

MAKES ENOUGH FOR 1 PIE

1/2 teaspoon powdered gelatin
1 tablespoon cold water
1 1/2 cups heavy cream

2 tablespoons sugar
1/2 teaspoon coconut extract

In a small saucepan over low heat, sprinkle the gelatin over the water and heat the water to melt the gelatin. In a mixing bowl, whip the cream and sprinkle in the sugar. As the cream begins to whip, drizzle in the gelatin and coconut extract.

Note: Because there is gelatin in this cream to stabilize it, you must spread it on the pie before the gelatin sets as it chills. Have the pie ready for this step before making the cream topping.

Banana Custard Sauce

MAKES 2 ¼ CUPS

5 egg yolks
½ cup sugar
2 cups heavy cream

½ vanilla bean, split lengthwise, or
   1 teaspoon pure vanilla extract
1 teaspoon banana extract

In a nonreactive stainless-steel bowl, whisk together the egg yolks and sugar. In a heavy-bottom saucepan over medium heat, heat the cream and vanilla bean until bubbles form around the edges. Slowly pour the hot cream into the egg yolk mixture, whisking constantly. Pour the mixture back into the saucepan. Gently cook over medium heat,

stirring constantly, until the sauce coats the back of a wooden spoon. Strain into a storage container. Take out the vanilla bean and scrape the vanilla bean seeds from the pod into the custard. Discard the vanilla bean. Add the banana extract and cool immediately in an ice bath. When fully cooled, cover and refrigerate. Serve cold.

Caramelized Bananas

MAKES 16 TO 24 BANANA SLICES

2 bananas
½ cup sugar

SPECIAL EQUIPMENT
Self-igniting propane torch

Slice the bananas on a bias, about ⅜ inch thick, and spread on a baking sheet. Sprinkle with the sugar and use a self-igniting

propane torch to caramelize the sugar. Serve immediately.

Mocha Chocolate Mousse with Whipped Cream

SERVES 4

This recipe is the ultimate. Chocolate lovers, meet your match!

7 ounces good quality semisweet
  chocolate, chopped
3 eggs yolks
⅓ cup honey
2 cups heavy cream

2 teaspoons espresso powder
2 tablespoons Kahlúa
Whipped Cream (page 200), for garnishing
Cocoa powder, for garnishing

In a stainless-steel bowl, melt the chocolate over a heated pot of water to create a double boiler; remove from the heat and set aside. In a standing mixer, whip the egg yolks on medium speed. In a very small saucepan, bring the honey to a boil. Remove the foam from the honey and discard it, then slowly pour the hot honey into the yolks. Continue whipping until the yolk mixture has tripled in volume. Fold the yolk mixture into the melted chocolate, which should be cooled but still velvety. Set aside.

In a mixing bowl, stir together the cream, espresso powder, and Kahlúa; until the espresso powder dissolves. Whip on medium speed until the cream doubles in volume and is smooth and creamy. If you whip the cream too much, the mousse may become grainy.

Fold half of the whipped cream mixture into the chocolate mixture until fully incorporated. Fold in the remaining whipped cream mixture and fully incorporate. Divide the mousse among 4 glasses and refrigerate. You may also pipe or spoon the mousse into Short Dough pastry shells (see page 203).

Serve with a dollop of whipped cream and a sprinkle of cocoa powder.

Chocolate Chip Pecan Pie with Bourbon Sauce

MAKES 1 (10-INCH) PIE

If you think nothing can make a pecan pie more delicious, think again! The addition of chocolate chips and bourbon sauce makes this recipe utterly decadent. I like to make this pie in the fall when the pecans are just starting to fall off the trees. It's the perfect dessert for your holiday table.

4 eggs, room temperature
$1/2$ cup plus 2 tablespoons sugar
1 cup dark corn syrup
1 tablespoon pure vanilla extract
6 tablespoons unsalted butter,
    melted and kept warm

$1\,1/2$ cups chopped pecans
$3/4$ cup good quality semisweet
    chocolate chips
1 (10-inch) unbaked Simple
    Pie Crust (page 34)
Bourbon Sauce (page 213)

Preheat the oven to 350 degrees F.

On the bottom rack of the oven, place a heavy baking sheet for 5 minutes before putting the pie in the oven. This provides extra heat to help the bottom crust brown.

In a large bowl, whisk together the eggs, sugar, corn syrup, and vanilla extract. Scrape the side and bottom of the bowl at least twice while mixing. Add the warm butter and mix well. In a separate bowl, combine the pecans and chocolate chips and sprinkle them on the bottom of the pie shell. Pour the filling over the nuts and chips.

Place the pie on the baking sheet and bake for 30 minutes. Move the pie to the middle shelf and continue to bake it for another 15 to 20 minutes. The edges of the filling will rise, but the middle will still be a little bouncy. However, the pie will continue to bake after it is removed from the oven. In order for the pie to be firm enough to slice, allow it to cool for 2 to 3 hours. Drizzle with bourbon sauce to serve.

Southern Pecan Pie with Bourbon Caramel Sauce

MAKES 1 (9-INCH) PIE

Looking back over the past thirty-plus years, this is Magnolias' second-most requested recipe! We keep our customers happy and have shipped these pies all across the country. Now you have the secret to making this outstanding pie at home.

3 eggs
1/2 cup dark brown corn syrup
1/2 cup light corn syrup
1/4 cup sugar
1/2 cup (1 stick) butter, melted
Pinch salt

1 teaspoon vanilla extract
1 (9-inch) unbaked Simple Pie
   Crust (page 34)
2 cups pecans, lightly toasted
Vanilla ice cream, for serving
Bourbon Caramel Sauce (page 211)

Preheat the oven to 350 degrees F.

In a medium bowl, whisk together the eggs, corn syrups, sugar, butter, salt, and vanilla. Place the pie shell in a 9-inch pie pan and trim off any excess, allowing enough to crimp the edges for a decorative crust. Spread the pecans in the bottom of the pie shell, then pour in the filling. Bake for 50 minutes, or until the

continued »

filling has set. Be sure to rotate the pie halfway through cooking. Allow the pie to cool at room temperature for at least 1 hour, or refrigerate until cool before cutting. Serve with vanilla ice cream and bourbon caramel sauce.

Bourbon Caramel Sauce

MAKES 2 TO 3 CUPS

1½ cups granulated sugar
⅓ cup water
3 tablespoons butter

1½ cups heavy (whipping) cream
2 tablespoons bourbon
Pinch salt

In a medium, heavy-bottom saucepan, combine the sugar and water. This is the only time you need to stir the sugar; otherwise, crystallization can occur. Also, make sure there is no sugar on the inside edges of the pot to prevent crystallization.

Place the saucepan over medium to low heat until the sugars start to dissolve, 5 to 10 minutes. Turn the heat up to medium-high and cook until the sugar starts to caramelize, 5 to 7 minutes. The mixture will be an amber color, similar to tea. Do not stir while this is happening. Watch the pot closely, because it goes from caramel to burnt quickly. Turn off the heat and stand back to avoid splattering. Slowly add the butter and cream. Don't panic—the cream will bubble violently, and the caramel might solidify. Simmer over low heat, stirring constantly until the caramel dissolves and the sauce is smooth, about 1 minute. Add the bourbon and salt and allow the sauce to cool to room temperature. It will thicken as it sits. The caramel sauce can be cooled more quickly with an ice bath.

Mama Squirrel's Sweet Potato Pie with White Chocolate and Bourbon Sauce

MAKES 1 (10-INCH) PIE

Charrette Jupiter, aka "Mama Squirrel," was a Magnolias pastry chef in the early 1990s. This is her interpretation of an Uptown Down South sweet potato pie. It's decadent and can't be beat!

3 pounds sweet potatoes
1 to 2 tablespoons vegetable oil
Nonstick cooking spray
1 (10-inch) unbaked Simple
    Pie Crust (page 34)
1 1/4 cups plus 3 tablespoons light
    brown sugar, divided
1 egg

1/4 cup whole milk
1/2 teaspoon ground cinnamon
1/4 teaspoon ground nutmeg
1 tablespoon pure vanilla extract
1 cup chunks or pieces of white
    chocolate (about 7 ounces)
Bourbon Sauce (recipe follows)

Preheat the oven to 400 degrees F.

Rub the sweet potatoes with vegetable oil, then pierce each potato once or twice with a fork to let the interior steam escape. Bake in the oven for 45 minutes to 1 hour, or until the potatoes are soft. Remove the potatoes and allow them to cool. Once the potatoes are cool enough to handle, peel them.

Reduce the oven to 350 degrees F.

Grease a 10-inch pie pan with nonstick cooking spray and place the pie shell in the pan. Gently pinch the edges of the shell for a decorative crust.

Place a heavy baking sheet on the bottom rack of the oven 5 minutes before putting the pie in the oven. This will provide extra heat to help brown the bottom crust.

Using an electric mixer with a flat paddle attachment, mix the potatoes and 1 1/4 cups of brown sugar to mash until smooth. Scrape the sides and the bottom of the bowl at least twice while mixing. Add the egg and blend in. Add the milk, cinnamon, nutmeg, and vanilla. Mix well to combine. Fold in the white chocolate chunks.

Pour the filling into the pie shell and spread evenly. Sprinkle the top with the remaining 3 tablespoons of brown sugar. Place the pie on the baking sheet on the bottom shelf of the oven. Bake for 20 minutes, then move the pan to the middle shelf and continue to bake for 30 to 40 minutes, or until the crust is golden and the filling is slightly puffed.

Remove the pie from the oven and let cool to room temperature before slicing. Serve with bourbon sauce.

Bourbon Sauce

2 sticks unsalted butter, diced
1 cup plus 2 tablespoons firmly
    packed dark brown sugar

$1/2$ cup heavy cream
$1/4$ cup bourbon

In a heavy-bottom saucepan over medium heat, warm the butter and brown sugar, whisking continuously for 5 to 10 minutes, or until the butter melts and the sugar is completely dissolved.

Slowly whisk in the cream, followed by the bourbon. Use at once or let cool to room temperature, pour into a storage container, and refrigerate for up to 1 week.

To rewarm the sauce, stir it over simmering water in a double boiler or over very low heat. If the heat is too high, the sauce may separate.

Key Lime Pie

The hardest question you'll have to ask ahead of this recipe is, "Do I want to make the crust or buy one?" They both work great, but the homemade crust is super easy and just tastes better. Secondly, do you want to just use Nellie & Joe's Key lime juice from the store, or squeeze the limes yourself? Your call!

There is a little seafood shop out on the Isle of Palms named Simmons Seafood. They have a Key lime pie made with sweetened condensed milk, eggs, and lime juice, with a graham cracker crust. I love their pie's simplicity, but knew I could improve it a little more with the addition of egg whites. Just don't tell Bubba!

GRAHAM CRACKER CRUMB CRUST

1½ cups finely ground graham cracker
　crumbs (about 1 sleeve of crackers)
3 tablespoons sugar
¼ teaspoon salt
6 tablespoons butter, melted
　and cooled a little

KEY LIME PIE FILLING

3 large eggs, separated
1 (14-ounce) can sweetened condensed milk
Zest of 1 lime
⅓ cup lime juice
¼ teaspoon salt

To make the graham cracker crumb crust: Preheat the oven to 350 degrees F. In a large mixing bowl, combine the graham cracker crumbs, sugar, and salt; mix well. Stir in the melted butter and mix until well combined.

Using a 9-inch pie pan, evenly press the crust filling around the pan. Place in the oven and bake for 10 minutes or until set. Remove from the oven. I like to refrigerate it for a little while before adding the filling.

To make the Key lime pie filling: Lower the oven to 300 degrees F. While the shell is cooling, beat the egg whites in a small mixing bowl until stiff peaks have formed.

In another bowl, lightly whisk the egg yolks. Add the condensed milk, lime zest, lime juice, and salt and mix until well combined. Gently fold in the beaten egg whites.

Pour the mixture into the cooled crust and bake for 15 minutes. Remove from the oven to cool and refrigerate for 2 hours or more before serving.

Resources

ASSORTED ITEMS/
WHOLESALE PRICES
US Foods Chef'Store
3304 Eastway Drive
Charlotte, North Carolina 28205
(704) 531–4610
ChefStore.com

CAROLINA PLANTATION
AROMATIC RICE
Carolina Plantation Rice
1515 Mont Clare Road
Darlington, South Carolina 29532
(877) 742–3496
CarolinaPlantationRice.com

CAST IRON AND CARBON
STEEL COOKWARE
Smithey Ironware Company
1465 Pipefitter Street
North Charleston, South Carolina 29405
(843) 619–0082
Smithey.com

DUKE'S MAYONNAISE
Sauer Brands, Inc.
2000 West Broad Street
Richmond, Virginia 23220
DukesMayo.com

MAGNOLIAS STONE GROUND GRITS
Magnolias
185 East Bay Street
Charleston, South Carolina 29401
(843) 577–7771
MagnoliasCharleston.com

PORK BUTTS, BACON,
HAM TRIMMINGS
Benton's Smoky Mountain Country Hams
2603 Highway 411 North
Madisonville, Tennessee 37354
(423) 442–5003
BentonsCountryHams2.com

Lee's Sausage Company, Inc.
1054 Neeses Highway
Orangeburg, South Carolina 29115
(803) 534-5517

TASSO HAM
D'Artagnan, LLC
600 Green Lane
Union, New Jersey 07083
Dartagnan.com

SPECIALTY PRODUCE, BEANS, PEAS, AND LETTUCES
The Chef's Garden
9009 Huron Avery Road
Huron, Ohio 44839
(419) 433-4947
Chefs-Garden.com

SPECIALTY PRODUCE, GRITS, AND BEANS
Limehouse Produce
2660 Corner Avenue
North Charleston, South Carolina 29405
(843) 556-3400
LimehouseProduce.com

SPECIALTY SEAFOOD (FISH, SOFT SHELL CRAB, CRAWFISH TAILS)
Crosby's Seafood Co.
2223 Folly Road
Charleston, South Carolina 29412
(843) 577-3531
CrosbysSeafood.com

Triar Seafood Company
2046 McKinley Street
Hollywood, Florida 33020
(954) 921-1113
TriarSeafood.com

STONE-GROUND GRITS
Marsh Hen Mill
2995 Highway 174
Edisto Island, South Carolina 29438
(843) 603-0074
MarshHenMill.com

WHITE LILY FLOUR
The White Lily Foods Company
1867 Dr. F. E. Wright Drive
Jackson, Tennessee 38301
1 (800) 595-1380
WhiteLily.com

Index

Metric Conversion Chart

Volume Measurements		Weight Measurements		Temperature Conversion	
U.S.	METRIC	U.S.	METRIC	FAHRENHEIT	CELSIUS
1 teaspoon	5 ml	½ ounce	15 g	250	120
1 tablespoon	15 ml	1 ounce	30 g	300	150
¼ cup	60 ml	3 ounces	90 g	325	160
⅓ cup	75 ml	4 ounces	115 g	350	180
½ cup	125 ml	8 ounces	225 g	375	190
⅔ cup	150 ml	12 ounces	350 g	400	200
¾ cup	175 ml	1 pound	450 g	425	220
1 cup	240 ml	2¼ pounds	1 kg	450	230